HAUNTED WARREN AIR FORCE BASE

HAUNTED WARREN AIR FORCE BASE

JILL POPE

Haunted America

Published by Haunted America
A Division of The History Press
Charleston, SC 29403
www.historypress.net

Cover images courtesy of Lisa Kindel.

First published 2014

Manufactured in the United States

ISBN 978.1.62619.562.2

Library of Congress CIP data applied for.

Dedicated to my loved ones who have passed away.
I miss you deeply but feel you around me, which is of great comfort.

CONTENTS

ACKNOWLEDGEMENTS

I'd like to express my sincere gratitude to everyone who graciously shared their paranormal encounters with me.

Heartfelt thanks and credit go to Valerie Martin—a fellow ghost enthusiast who created the trolley ghost tours and has a deep loyalty and passion for them. Many of the stories in this book were acquired by Val pre-9/11, when the trolleys did daily tours on Warren Air Force Base (WAFB). I'd also like to recognize all of the Cheyenne Street Railway Trolley drivers and guides who represent Cheyenne so well.

I would like to thank Cheyenne Paranormal Investigations (CPI), with whom I've worked over the years. The team that participated in the base investigation in 2007 includes Troy Brandt, founder and original team leader; Scott Newbury, founding member; Brenda Middleton; Natasha Middleton; and K. "Creeps" Holden. Investigators Larry and Joe joined in the 2007 WAFB investigation. CPI members who did the 2008 WAFB paranormal investigations included Bob Aquin, second team leader; Jessica Garcia; Dylan; Troy Delois; and Roy. Other CPI members are Stacie Tomlinson, Amy Lambert, Sara Aquin and Leslie Aquin.

I'd also like to thank Rocky Mountain Paranormal Research Society: Bryan Bonner, Matthew Baxter, Stu Hayes and Carol Olivacz (www.rockymountainparanormal.com).

Appreciation goes to Alex Martinez (2007–08) from Public Affairs–Community Relations for Base for his assistance and to Lieutenant Myman and Lieutenant Knee of Public Affairs (2007). Dan Lyon, base historian

(2009), gave me continued assistance with trolley tour historical information and a base tour. Recently, in preparation for this book, I was assisted by Eydie Sakura, first lieutenant, U.S. Air Force Global Strike Command 90 Missile Wing/Public Affairs, and Christen Ornella, second lieutenant, U.S. Air Force Global Strike Command 90 Missile Wing/Public Affairs, as well as Paula Bauman Taylor, base historian and Intercontinental Ballistic Missile and Heritage Museum curator, and James Fuller, historian.

With much love to all of my family and friends, thank you for the support. Special acknowledgement to my nephew Chris Larson, whom I neglected to mention in my first book. I shall not make that mistake again!

Special acknowledgements to all of the Visit Cheyenne staff for the continuous support and encouragement. Lisa Kindel, thanks for being the book photographer—you do great work.

INTRODUCTION

With cable television airing nonstop reality shows, we have been inundated with material on the supernatural. Whether it's aliens, sasquatches or psychic or spiritual activity, there is no shortage of information pouring into our households and heads. While some of the propaganda seems quite preposterous, all this has made these subjects more approachable. People are willing to tell about their paranormal experiences, and the general public is becoming open to the possibilities. My generation and many before it were programmed to think within the box—color within the lines. We were taught that there were no such thing as ghosts. We tend to try and rationalize our paranormal experiences, as we should, because there is often a scientific answer. My advice is to keep an open mind; it may lead somewhere quite fascinating. Spirits reach out to us in ways that we don't understand.

I am the director of the Cheyenne Street Railway trolleys as part of my position as director of operations at Visit Cheyenne, where we promote tourism in Cheyenne and Laramie County in Wyoming. The first trolley tours began in 1988, and the base was included in the general Cheyenne historic tour. The trolley ran daily historic tours on the base in the summer until security issues from 9/11 prevented its entrance onto the base. The tours still run seven days a week in the summer, traveling through the historic neighborhoods of Cheyenne, excluding WAFB. The trolley guides, mainly Valerie Martin and her father, Bob Morgan, weren't even looking for ghosts in the early trolley days. When they met base residents during their daily

Cheyenne trolley on the fort, circa 1920s. *Courtesy of Visit Cheyenne photo collection.*

tours, they would ask them about the history of their homes. More often than not, they received a ghost story in reply. The duo became fascinated with the ghosts of Warren Air Force Base and documented the accounts.

I became the manager of the Cheyenne Street Railway trolleys in 2002, less than a year after 9/11. While the trolleys are occasionally chartered for a tour on the base, we do not have the daily access to the post or its stories that we once had. Several of the stories I have compiled here came from the tour guides who drove the trolley prior to 2001. Valerie Martin is the source of many of these stories and has been a trolley guide for over twenty years, since 1993. She is quite an asset to our trolley program. Val's father, Bob Morgan, used to be a trolley driver as well. He passed away some years after he retired from driving the trolleys. The two of them created the ghost tours, wrote all the original scripts and are responsible for much of the material presented in this book. There were other trolley guides who participated and helped grow the tours. I have been actively collecting additional tales of the supernatural on the base and in the city of Cheyenne since I started working for Visit Cheyenne and Cheyenne Street Railway in 2002. It's become quite a passion and is definitely the most enjoyable part of my job. Whenever I meet someone who works or lives on the base, I question him or her about paranormal experiences. While I expect people to think I'm flaky at the inquiry, the majority of them reply with a ghost story or two, many of them saying they did not believe in such nonsense until they experienced the paranormal themselves at Warren Air Force Base.

Because many stories are told to me by second- or third-hand parties, I don't always have a lot of details about the person who actually experienced the event. A number of the stories shared with us happened to the

Valerie Martin, Cheyenne Street Railway tour guide. *Courtesy of Matt Idler Photography.*

people we interviewed a decade or more ago. It is not possible to locate the majority of them, although I would love to visit with them to learn more about their experiences. As these stories were gathered over the years, we told these individuals that we wouldn't use their real names. While I believe our society is becoming much more open to the supernatural, and 75 percent of the people surveyed in the United States believe in the paranormal, there are still people who are embarrassed to admit that they have confronted or believe in the paranormal. That is even more true on a dignified military base. I have written as many details as I could for each story in order to give you the full picture of each event. Please note that most of the names used for the individuals who shared their stories are not real, as we promised them anonymity.

Most individuals who serve in the military are strong, no-nonsense types of people, both emotionally and physically. We expect that of them. These are the people protecting our freedoms. It stands to reason that when people pass over to the other side, into the next dimension, they retain their same personalities. They have surely gained new insights from the transition but are basically the same people that they were here on earth; they just don't reside in their physical bodies any longer. It makes sense that these strong military personalities can be sensed by humans. The spirits of those who have passed in traumatic and devastating ways are often witnessed; the intense energy of the strong emotions accompanying these deaths is perceived by our sixth sense. That phrase, "listen to your gut," is telling you to listen to that sixth sense—trust your instincts and intuition. Many strong spirit presences are felt on Warren Air Force Base, especially in the historic buildings. That does not mean that a presence won't ever be felt in a newer building. Every single inch of our earth has a history. Any spot can retain some residual energy from days gone by. The location of a brand-new building could also be the exact location where a pioneer dropped to his death from the elements. According to an F.E. Warren Archaeology brochure, evidence of Native American life here on the post has been found, dating back as far as 11,500 years ago. They were Paleo-Indians. The fire pit uncovered in the FamCamp on the west side of the base is 1,600 years old. In the spring, the people traveled along Crow Creek up into the mountains to enjoy the cool weather and then back down to the plains for the winters.

When spirits make themselves known and display no signs of malice or animosity, I think the witnesses should feel flattered. These spirits are sharing their presence with them. In some cases, the spirits help uncover truths, tell their life stories or guide living humans in their own life choices. It is not always just happenstance when a spirit shows itself. It may be sending a message—pay close attention.

In many of the interviews I've done for trolley ghost tours, Haunted Cheyenne and this haunted WAFB book, the individuals say they never believed in ghosts until they had notable paranormal experiences themselves. While this makes sense, I don't personally relate to that statement. I cannot remember a time when I didn't believe in ghosts, and I have always been extremely curious about things we cannot explain.

I
FYI

Paranormal Investigations

I have aligned with paranormal investigators over the years during the process of creating our annual trolley ghost tours. My first consultation was with Troy Brandt, who founded CPI (Cheyenne Paranormal Investigations). It didn't take us long to realize this was a great partnership. I love doing the research, and the CPI team delves into the science. I am not an expert in paranormal investigating; I just surround myself with those who are.

Investigation equipment and techniques are constantly evolving, as is all technology. While there is so much more out there than we can measure, it's worth the effort to try. Paranormal investigators take environmental readings—which can simultaneously take visual and audio recordings at a variety of frequencies—of the site and other readings, including ambient temperature; electromagnetic field fluctuations (EMF); electronic voice phenomenon (EVP); detecting sounds the naked ear cannot hear; and atmospheric readings of barometric pressure, relative humidity, dew point and ionization levels. Laser grids detect movement and help define the entity. Large fluctuations in these readings can sometimes be attributed to spirit energy, when all factors are considered and other causes ruled out. There are many tools used in investigations, such as DVRs (digital still cameras with high resolution so you can zoom in tight), thermal imaging cameras (which detect temperature variations) and static full spectrum night vision cameras (which allow us to see infrared light beyond our normal sight). They can shoot and record in darkness.

Baseline readings need to be taken prior to any investigation to determine normal levels of electrical energy. Any electrical equipment and appliances plugged in will create energy, as will wiring and nearby power lines. The readings can vary just from having the lights turned on or off. When there are fluctuations in the readings, further investigation needs to be done to see if there is an explanation for the change.

I caution people to do their research before delving into the paranormal. Be careful what you summon. Anyone can go online and buy a paranormal investigation kit. There's an old saying that someone "knows just enough to be dangerous." This statement can be very true. At least one person on the investigative team needs to be science-minded and have a strong understanding of basic scientific principles. If not, many happenings might be falsely attributed to paranormal activity. As simple examples of this, orbs—which are light specs that are seen in photographs or video clips—are most often caused by dust particles in the air, and sometimes they are reflections from the camera's flash. Shutter speeds also affect photographs. Many EVPs are simply picked up from surrounding radio bands. EMF readings are accurate only if the tester is moving slowly with no jerking movements. A space can be affected by low-vibration sound emissions. These vibrations can be caused by a variety of sources, mainly machinery and equipment—for instance, sump pumps and fans. So while a person cannot actually hear these vibrations, or they hear a very low hum, it has been proven that the low-frequency tones can negatively affect people. They can cause symptoms such as headaches; stomachaches; eye, ear, throat and chest irritations; nervousness; aggressive behavior; depression; and even hallucinations. Quite often, symptoms caused from low vibrations are attributed to paranormal activity when it's simply not so.

CPI conducted three investigations into the many paranormal sightings on the base and allowed me join it for the first one in 2007. It returned two more times in 2008. We investigated Building 34, Security Forces Ninetieth Missile Wing (the former hospital); Building 37, Special Forces Investigations; Building 214, the Base Library; and Building 233, the Civil Air Patrol. CPI also investigated a colonel's quarters, Building 73. The results of these investigations will be included in this book. For me, the best part of being included in the base investigations was the opportunity to meet and interview the staff members in these buildings. I gathered many more stories and had a splendid time doing it.

FYI

Spirit boxes were not yet used at the time of these investigations. Spirit boxes are controversial in the paranormal researcher's world. Many investigators are skeptical of spirit boxes, which were designed specifically for paranormal investigations to enhance communication. They are said to capture audio in real time, reaching far beyond the human ear's range. They use radio frequency sweeps to generate white noise that provides energy for the spirit to manifest sound that our ears cannot hear on their own. This can be immediately played back, which makes the investigation much more efficient, according to the believers. Skeptics say that the device picks up frequencies from other broadcasting devices like radios and CBs.

I met with Rocky Mountain Paranormal Research Society (RMPRS) while working on this book. It had done an investigation on Warren Air Force Base in January 2006. Its members were kind enough to share their investigation's findings with me and allow me to include them in this book. RMPRS has been together since 1999, and it is quite established in the field. The group prides itself on exposing hoaxes. Team members have training in computer science, photography and video editing, electronics, digital audio and imaging and graphic arts, with certifications in electromagnetic field surveying, hypnosis and forensic hypnotherapy, thermal imaging, OSHA inspections, business management, world religions and countless other certifications from which they draw during their investigations. Most tools used in paranormal investigating were developed for other scientific studies. Team members Bryan and Baxter conveyed to me the importance of being trained in operating these devices in the purposes for which they were created, resulting in a more full understanding of the science and therefore more accurate conclusions. They strongly believe that spirit boxes do not work. Bryan and Baxter of RMPRS have been featured on *Larry King Live*, Peter Boyles's morning show, *Fox News*, *The Scariest Places on Earth*, *Is It Real*, *The Most Terrifying Places on Earth* and *Ghost Hunters*. Bryan has conducted classes and presentations nationally on aspects of the pseudoscientific realm.

A Taste of History: Army to Air Force

Francis E. Warren Air Force Base is located on the west side of Cheyenne, Wyoming, just three miles from downtown. It is the oldest active military post in the United States and is the only active federal military installation in Wyoming. This post has been continuously active since it was originally established in 1867, and it is steeped with history of the generations of servicemen who have dwelled here.

The base is highly populated with ghosts despite the fact that the post was never attacked, nor was there ever a military battle fought there, although the men were involved in various off-site battles and Indian engagements, including the Great Sioux Indian Wars in 1876. This is the same war in which Custer was defeated. The history is strong at WAFB, and the spirits of many remain to tell their tales.

Here's an abbreviated history of the post so that you can better understand the spirits that reside here. Fort D.A. Russell, an army fort, was the predecessor to Warren Air Force Base at the same location. Fort Russell was established at the same time as the town of Cheyenne in 1867. General Auger, working along with General Grenville Dodge, selected the location of the fort. In July 1867, the railroad gang pitched its tents and set up a makeshift town along the banks of Crow Creek. The tent city included many saloons. The men worked hard during the day and played hard at night. Fort Russell was established under the orders of Abraham Lincoln to protect the railroad workers from hostile Indians who had free run of the prairie before their arrival. The fort was named for General David A. Russell, who perished in battle the very day he was appointed major general. The hardy soldiers arrived in Cheyenne in October and November 1867. They lived in pup tents until their wooden hut quarters were completed in February 1868. Winter out on the prairie in Cheyenne is not conducive to tent life. Camp Carlin, a supply depot, was set up just south of the fort to provide supplies to the soldiers and railroaders.

Four-star general Ulysses S. Grant inspected the post in July 1868, exactly one year following the selection of the Cheyenne and Fort D.A. Russell sites. Grant was there on official military business, but he was also campaigning for his upcoming role as president of the United States, which he acquired the following year.

Eventually, the fort became the largest cavalry post in the United States. In 1884, the post was declared a permanent military installation because of the value of its location, strategically positioned along the railroad halfway between Mexico and Canada and nearly the midpoint between Los Angeles and New York. The makeshift wooden buildings that had been put up were replaced by twenty-seven sturdier, one-story, light redbrick structures. The soldiers planted trees and put out fifty bushels of grass seed on the prairie, which they now called home. Some of the old wooden houses were moved into Cheyenne. A handful still exist in town today. We have ghost stories about some of them—one where the residents often see a soldier in a blue uniform who apparently accompanied his home into town. They often catch his reflection in mirrors throughout the home. Their four-year-old nephew sees him and refers to him as George.

It was another six years after the post was designated a permanent installation before Wyoming was declared a state. Prior to 1890, it had been the Wyoming Territory. In 1898, President McKinley sent soldiers to Cuba and the Philippines during the Spanish-American War. In 1901, the troops were once again sent to the Philippines to bring peace to the area.

After the turn of the century, Fort Russell survived the threat of closure in 1901, and an expansion was done beginning in 1902 through 1914 to include an infantry regiment and artillery battery. Nearly two hundred more substantial two-story dark redbricks were erected, most of them along Randall Avenue. They are still used to this day.

Troops from Fort Russell were stationed along the southern border of the United States during the Mexican Revolution (1913–16). From 1914 to 1918, the base served as a training facility and mobilization point during World War I. It was one of the largest military posts in the United States at the time.

The year 1927 marks the removal of the last cavalry unit assigned to Warren Air Force Base after sixty years at the post. In January 1930, the president renamed the installation Fort Francis E. Warren, honoring the beloved Warren, who had served in the Civil War and as a United States

A soldier at the post after the turn of the century. *Courtesy of Warren ICBM Heritage Museum.*

senator from Wyoming for thirty-seven years. Warren was also Wyoming's last territorial governor and the state of Wyoming's very first governor. Warren had always been a strong advocate of the installation and had helped keep it open in times of question. Warren died while still in office in 1929, at the age of eighty-five; he was the last Civil War veteran in Congress. Warren is buried in Cheyenne's Lakeview Cemetery.

Troops trained at this army fort during World War II. A quartermaster training center was operated there during the war, from 1940 to 1946. A quartermaster is a soldier or a unit that specializes in distributing supplies and provisions to troops. Nearly three hundred wooden buildings were slapped up for temporary housing for these troops on the south banks of Crow Creek. The makeshift buildings did not have insulation, and the soldiers often had snow inside their dwellings. The base population was twenty-six thousand at this time. The houses were torn down in the 1950s after being declared unfit for use. On a fun note, Bing Crosby visited the post with a USO group to entertain for two days in the summer of 1941.

In 1947, after the war, the air force became its own branch of the military, and in two years, the fort was transformed into an air force base, although it has never had an airport. There was a lone, rough airstrip in 1919–20, but it was closed when Cheyenne opened an airport. World War I flying ace Eddie Rickenbacher crashed on this dirt runway in 1920 but lived to tell about it. The fort was used as a training facility for the next decade, offering studies in aviation, engineering and administration.

In 1958, the mission of the base shifted to missiles, beginning with twenty-four Atlas missiles. After two years, they were replaced by Minuteman I missiles. These were updated in the 1970s with the Minuteman III, and in 1975, the Peacekeeper missile system was installed. WAFB was the only base in the nation that maintained the Peacekeeper. There were fifty Peacekeepers in the region. Warren Air Force Base was the most powerful military installation during the cold war. Fortunately, a missile was never launched.

Security police were stationed at the main gate once the missiles arrived; the general public was no longer free to access the post without clearance. Approximately 265 housing units were built in 1987, south of the original fort structures.

Warren Air Force Base is the home of the Twentieth Air Force and the Ninetieth Missile Wing, both major presences in our nation's military defense. The Twentieth Air Force controls operations of the intercontinental ballistic missile wings, and the Ninetieth Missile Wing's mission maintained and kept alert 150 Minuteman III missiles in Wyoming, Nebraska and

Colorado. From 1987 to 2005, the Peacekeeper missiles were operational. In accordance with the Strategic Arms Reduction Treaty (START), the missile system was deactivated in 2005.

Warren Air Force Base has ties to a couple celebrities. When Sammy Davis Jr. turned eighteen, he was drafted into the United States Army and was sent to basic training at WAFB. Davis was transferred to an entertainment regiment and was soon performing to the cheers of those who had previously treated him with prejudice. Famous pop singer Neil Diamond moved to Cheyenne when he was four years old. His father was stationed at Warren Air Force Base during World War II. They lived there until the war was over and then moved back to Brooklyn when Neil was fifteen years old.

Enter at Your Own Risk

When passing through the prestigious brick arch at the main gate, you feel a proud surge of patriotism while observing the three impressive missiles postured as though they are standing at attention against the sprawling Wyoming sky. As mentioned earlier, Warren Air Force Base is home to the Twentieth Air Force and the Ninetieth Missile Wing. Randall Avenue is the main thoroughfare from the city of Cheyenne to the post, passing through

Missiles standing at attention beside WAFB's main gate. *Courtesy of Public Affairs.*

the main gate and running the width of the base. The street is lined with orderly redbrick buildings in military precision that have stood there for over a century, all with stories to tell.

The boundary of the post is surrounded by fencing. A female spirit appearing in light-colored attire anxiously paces the fence line near the main gate. Military police are often summoned to check on her suspicious behavior, but they never find anyone on their arrival.

ARGONNE PARADE FIELD

Journeying into the post, you soon see the beautiful Argonne Parade Field blanketed in green grass, with stately brick officers' homes encircling the northern half. More often than not, you'll spot a herd of antelope contentedly grazing on the field and throughout the base. They are tended to by the natural resources unit of the civil engineers squadron. The parade field was originally used for artillery purposes. It has served various purposes over the past century. If there was not enough room in the barracks, the soldiers pitched tents on the parade field. In the mornings, the army would disseminate orders and do physical training from here. Until 1986, it functioned as a polo field, which was quite popular at most army posts. Currently, military ceremonies and reviews, as well as parades and sporting events, are held here. An exercise track was created around the perimeter for the base residents' benefit. There are six parade fields on the base, but this is the largest.

IMPRESSIONABLE BOYS

Cindy worked in a finance office on the base. She had her son Nick with her at the office one morning. They heard music drifting over from the Argonne Parade Field. Nick was curious, so he wandered over to check it out. As Nick approached the field, he beheld the full-bodied apparition of a young boy saluting the live soldiers. The boy's clothes were from a past era. Nick intently watched the young spirit, and after a few moments, the impression simply faded away, leaving Nick standing there in awe.

Phantom Maneuvers, Argonne Parade Field

An interesting note about the next story is that I personally interviewed "Kent" and was intrigued by his story. I could tell his experiences changed his perspectives on life hereafter. Kent has an essence that garners respect—a quality military officers strive for. While preparing for this book, I compiled all of the Warren Air Force Base information that we had accumulated in the office over the past twenty years. When sorting through it all, I found notes from 1998 that detailed the exact same ghost story. What I don't know is if Kent shared this story with another Cheyenne Street Railway employee fifteen years ago or if a second person experienced the same events in Building 129. Some paranormal events repeat themselves as if they are echoes from days gone by.

Kent, a retired air force officer, needed some assistance from Visit Cheyenne. While he was in our office in 2007, we began conversing about the base, which quickly led to talk of the many ghosts residing there. Kent had more than one story to share with me from his time at the base. Kent was put up at the building that sits beside the Argonne Parade Field and is designated as Visiting Officers' Quarters.

Cavalry maneuvers on the parade field. *Courtesy of Wyoming State Archives.*

At the dreadfully early hour of four o'clock in the morning, Kent was awakened by a commotion outside. He peered out the window and was bewildered to see cavalry tents and soldiers with their horses and even cannons set up on the parade grounds before him. Kent wondered why he hadn't been apprised of the maneuvers taking place just outside his accommodations. He thought it a very elaborate cavalry reenactment. Finally, Kent fell back to sleep despite the noise. Early the next morning, he inquired about the activity, but no one knew what he was talking about. Intent to prove that maneuvers had taken place during the night, he took some staff members to the parade grounds, but they were unable to find a shred of evidence to prove his case. There were no footprints or hoof prints, no tracks from the wagons pulling the heavy cannons and no holes in the ground from the tent stakes. Kent was deflated and embarrassed, but these unexplained sightings are a frequent occurrence on the base, so the staff took it in stride. The passions of those maneuvers a century past are imprinted in the parade field—the men marching endlessly into eternity. Kent was allowed a rare view into the past through these lingering remnants.

II
Housing

Presence of Danger, Quarters 129

There have been numerous sightings within the redbrick Visiting Officers' Quarters (VOQ) 129 where Kent stayed. When various people with no connections to one another experience the same events at a location, it does support the validity of the paranormal activity.

Building 129 has a mysterious air about it; it was constructed in 1910 to house ten bachelor officers. Most of the enlisted men weren't married then because the army didn't make suitable allowances for families at that time.

The United States Air Force Thunderbirds have stayed in these fine accommodations when they've come to perform at Cheyenne Frontier Days, a colossal annual rodeo festival. The military has been involved in Cheyenne Frontier Days every year since its inception in 1897. The VOQ building was renovated in the 1990s. The reopening was delayed because it was close to Halloween, so reenactments of its ghost stories were performed for the holiday.

In the murky basement, a lady in a flowing gown glides right through a bricked-up door, which is thought to be her former bedroom. Witnesses have seen her flowing right through a person who happened to be standing in her path, her arms wildly flailing about.

The apparition of a sullen elderly lady wearing black is often seen swaying back and forth in her rocking chair. She is seen in the sitting room that adjoined her bedroom, where she perished in her bed. The woman is said

Visiting Officers' Quarters. *Courtesy of Lisa Kindel.*

to be a blacksmith's wife; he was frequently away, and she was a lonely soul. Blacksmiths were responsible for shoeing the hundreds of pack mules and horses that moved all of the soldiers' supplies. This particular blacksmith's wife remains there in seclusion, awaiting the return of her husband.

The cavalry officer is often seen downstairs on the east side of Building 129, showing us fragments of his life. He is said to be one of the bachelors who lived there when the brick was first built. Apparently, he has some unfinished business and has chosen to stay on. He occupied two rooms; the back room was his office. There is a side door to his office. This area has been converted into a bedroom. Various visitors over the years report seeing an intimidating officer standing in the room with a look of disgust on his face. He repeatedly disturbs them when they try to sleep in the room. When he has their attention, he scowls and points to the door, indicating that they should get out. He resents them being there and wants to reclaim his office.

Todd, a visiting marine, woke up in a panicked state. The possessive cavalry officer's spirit had unleashed his fury. He was on Todd's chest brutally holding the marine down, and Todd could not move. Mustering all his strength, Todd flung himself from the bed and frantically ran away from this vengeful ghost. He darted outside and across the parade field wearing only his boxer briefs!

KEEP THE LIGHT ON FOR ME, QUARTERS 131

A police officer revealed that he and several colleagues would spot the beam of a lit lantern swinging inside of Building 131's front window. When one of the officers would walk up next to the glass and peer into the house, he could no longer see the lantern, but those who were still standing farther back could see the glow of the light swaying to and fro behind their co-worker's head.

BACHELOR PAD, QUARTERS 130

Building 130 has been converted into a fourplex. It was originally quarters for single or unaccompanied officers and was a big, open barracks with rows of twin beds lining the walls. A 1995 resident told us that as he stood in the kitchen, a loaf of bread went plunging off the counter of its own accord.

Fifteen years later, in 2010, the current resident said she didn't know how she provoked this spirit, but her furniture suddenly moved madly around the room as she stood helplessly by. With no control of the situation, she

Quad Quarters 130. *Courtesy of Lisa Kindel.*

desperately shouted, "Stop it!" and much to her relief, the movement ceased. She was standing there in the center of the room, not knowing what to do. She was afraid to sit down in the event that the furniture would move again. While the immediate danger was over, she never again felt completely comfortable in the home.

SLEEPWALKER, QUARTERS 124B

I recently attained the story of Quarters 124B, where the residents' daily lives are intertwined with those from another realm. This captain's family of five moved into their charming new home. As darkness fell, they were exhausted from the rigors of moving, and they all dropped into their beds and quickly drifted off. The excitement of a new home was short-lived. Tiffanie and Dan were shaken from their slumber at the loud thumping sounds of someone falling down a flight of stairs. Frightened that it was one of their three children, the couple bolted from their bed and rushed to the staircase, their hearts stopping for a few beats. Much to their relief, there was no one at the bottom of the stairs. They did a bed check and found their children safely tucked in their beds. That just left them standing there with no answers, no way to rationalize the sounds they had both heard—sounds loud enough to wake them. About a week later, the exact same thing happened again, jolting them out of a sound sleep for the second time. Both Dan and Tiffanie have noticed that there is an area on this staircase where there is an isolated cold spot; they feel uneasy when they walk through the space.

Katie, their eldest daughter, is sixteen and does not like paranormal things. The supernatural really frightens her. She timidly confided to her parents that she had woken up in the middle of the night and seen the apparition of a small girl with long, dark hair standing down the hallway. Katie retreated to her bed, shuddering. She closed her eyes tightly, denying what she had just witnessed. Her parents had not revealed to her any of their unexplained experiences because they knew it would really upset her, so this account was not encouraged by her parents.

One winter's night, Tiffanie could hear footsteps pacing back and forth, back and forth, on the creaky attic floor above her. She tried to credit the cats with the footsteps, but logically she knew that couldn't be. These were the sounds of heavy boots clunking overhead. The next morning, Tori, age fourteen, complained to her mother that she had not gotten any sleep the previous night. The loud footsteps kept her awake. Steven, who was ten years old, also heard footsteps directly above his bedroom with some frequency. They also noticed the cats would stare at something the rest of the family could not see.

Shedding new light on the situation, Katie accused her younger sister Tori of bothering her in the middle of the night, turning her lights on and off. Tori insisted she had not done so. Tori then shared an experience she had. She got up to use the bathroom when the rest of the family was asleep. While she was up, she glanced over at the mirror and was shocked to see a pale young girl staring back at her from the mirror next to her own reflection. She scurried back to her bed and nuzzled in, trying to calm herself. For nights, she lay there stressed in the dark.

A few months later, Tiffanie was standing at the kitchen counter preparing a meal. When she turned around, she was caught off guard to find a pile of plastic spoons stacked on the floor in the center of the room. She realized that these were the spoons that had been sitting in a container on top of the refrigerator. How in the world did the spoons move from the top of the refrigerator to the center of the kitchen floor? There was no sound when this happened.

The family has a radio in the kitchen that turns on and off with no assistance. This also happens with Tori's bedroom radio, and the DVR/cable box often turns off in the middle of a show.

After being in the house for a while, Tiffanie began feeling someone nudge her, trying to get her attention. She was often the only family member home. She also sees someone walk past in her peripheral vision. This happens at least once a day. Often, when sitting on the living room couch, she will glance down the hall and see someone move across the kitchen, but no one else is home. This was really frightening at first, but now she's come to expect it. She also sees a silhouette standing on the stairs.

The attic is a great hangout space for the kids and their friends. There is a nonfunctioning bathroom up there. The kids say the room creeps them out so they close the door. Every time they look, the door is wide open, so they close it again. This happens repeatedly. The whole family often hears doors banging shut up in the attic when none of them is up there. They have tried to discount it as the wind, but the house is closed up tight and it really doesn't compute.

Then something really bizarre happened. Tiffanie noticed something lying in the middle of the living room floor. Thinking one of her kids had left something there, she walked over and scooped it up. It was a chain with dog tags on it. Oddly, the name on the tags was that of an officer's son. He was a really nice boy, but while they were acquainted with the family, they did not interact with them much. After questioning everyone in the house, she found that no one had any answers for how the dog tags ended up in the living room. Their kids attended a different school from this boy, and they were not in any clubs or sports together. He had never been to their home. The captain brought the dog tags to the boy's father, who was equally perplexed. The boy was happy to get his dog tags back, but to this day, neither family has an explanation for how the dog tags ended up in a home a couple blocks away.

Despite the fact that they have a young sleepwalker spirit dwelling in their home that likes to make her presence known in the middle of the night, the family is both comfortable and honored to live in this distinguished house with so much history.

Sweet Tooth, Quarters 123

The tenants at Quarters 123 have a temperamental ghost that slams doors. They said that when they left candy sitting out, the ghost wasn't nearly as grumpy. A ghost with a sweet tooth—I must say, that is a new concept that I've not heard before!

The man who lived there was really edgy about the paranormal activity happening in his home. Before his marriage, he actually slept with every light in the house turned on but is a bit more comfortable now that he is not there alone. Safety in numbers must be his theory.

Picture Perfect, Quarters 122A

In 2010, Cheyenne Paranormal Investigations received a letter from Kara, who was experiencing paranormal activity in her residence at 122A. She gave the group permission to share the account with me.

On moving day, Kara was the first one at the house. She quickly became uneasy because it sounded like someone was furiously pacing around. It frightened her so much that she left, waiting to return when her husband could join her. On the day they moved in, they took a picture of Kara in the hallway of their new home. Kara was wearing a sweatshirt. There was a dark area on her left shoulder, which wasn't a stain or shadow. It caught their attention. They zoomed in and could see eyes, the face fading into the shirt. Later, Kara randomly took a picture in their living room, where she really experienced an intense energy. In the center of the photo, seen above the couch, is the eerie, white face of a woman. They snapped a picture of Kara and a girlfriend, and when they peered at the image in the camera screen they noticed a pronounced male face in the mirror behind them. They turned to look at the mirror but saw nothing unusual; however, the photo told a different story.

The second night the couple was in their house, they went to sleep in their newly set-up bed. They were awakened about midnight by music coming from the radio; it was playing old-time country western music. Kara groggily got up, trying not to make anything of it, and shut the stereo off. The next morning, she looked more closely at the radio to see if the sleep button had been pushed. She checked the knob; it was in the off position and would have had to have been turned on physically. She then checked the radio station. It wasn't even tuned to a country station.

Another night, Kara locked their cat out of the room because she was making noise. Two hours later, Kara woke up to sounds of things being rustled around on their dresser. She flipped the light on but found nothing.

Kara feels a presence around her nearly all of the time when she is in the house. She sees fleeting glimpses of something from the corner of her eye. Sometimes she endures the feeling of pins and needles prickling her arms and back. Other times, she feels an intense pressure in her head and a heaviness that forces her to leave the room—sometimes she has to leave the home entirely. Kara said she told the spirits to leave but still feels them there taunting her. She is trying to cohabitate with her unwanted guests. Some of the experiences Kara reports could be caused by low-frequency vibrations. As I explained in the "Paranormal Investigation" section at the beginning of this book, these vibrations can be caused by a variety of sources like machinery and equipment. So while a person usually does not hear the low-frequency tones, they can negatively affect some people. Events caused from low vibrations are sometimes attributed to paranormal activity. It would be prudent to take some readings at 122A. That would not explain the photographs, however. I have seen the photos. The first shot of Kara in her sweatshirt may or may not be paranormal—it's questionable. But there is something unusual appearing above the couch, and there is most definitely a person appearing in the mirror in the third shot. I wasn't there when these photographs were taken, but Kara assured CPI that no one was standing there beside the cameraman.

THE GAMES CHILDREN PLAY, QUARTERS 118A AND 117

A trolley passenger was fondly remembering her childhood living in Quarters 118A. She told the trolley guide that her little brother played with another little boy whom only he could see. Sure, maybe he had an imaginary friend, but maybe the boy was invisible rather than imaginary. It is said that children see spirits with much more frequency than adults before they are taught that there is no such thing. The family called the invisible boy George, and George didn't stop playing when the family was out. They'd come home to find the beds rumpled, decorative items out of place and the mother's makeup messed with. George even stole the father's trousers. It's hard enough to keep the house in order with your own children around, but try adding spirit children to the mix! A housekeeper may be in order.

Quarters 117 is one of three original commanding officers' homes and is said to have a boy ghost that is also called George. I speculate that it is the same spirit as in number 118, just wandering a bit, looking for playmates.

HORSE PLAY, QUARTERS 110B

Many of the base homes were built with horse stables in the basement. There were big double doors in the ground that pulled open, with stairs down which the horses could maneuver to the basement. While I have notations on two ghosts here, the most interesting comment is that they are accompanied by a horse. It's been fifty-five years since a horse was boarded here, yet the residents at 110 smell and hear a horse in their home on occasion.

Quarters 110. *Courtesy of Lisa Kindel.*

MOONSHINE, QUARTERS 108

There is a smoldering story of an explosion at Quarters 108, one of the two historic quad housing units on base, originally built in 1911 to house four officers who were bachelors.

I have a photocopy of the maintenance report for this building and have confirmed that an explosion happened at this spot on September 28, 1921. The bachelors set up an illegal still in the basement since this was during Prohibition. Unfortunately, the still exploded, and the entire east wall of the complex blew over as result. Repairs from the fire cost nearly $30,000 in 1921. This was more than the cost of the original construction of the building a decade earlier. Two young lieutenants' lives were snuffed out in the devastating moonshine fire. We have a number of reports that at least one of these lieutenants remains here. A heavy antique dresser is frequently pushed up against a door, blocking the entrance to the room. There is no one inside of the room, so residents question how this happens. A woman on a Warren Air Force Base spouses trolley tour told us she has heard that there is paranormal activity happening in the attic as well.

Frame of Mind, General's Quarters 92

The major general is the commander of the Twentieth Air Force and the highest-ranking officer at WAFB. As tradition would have it, he and his family live in Quarters 92, bordering Argonne Parade Field. This stately home was built from 1908 to 1910 and was designed by Charles Murdock, the same architect who designed Wyoming's Historic Governors' Mansion. Visitors are drawn to Quarters 92, a lovely Colonial Revival–style house made of red brick with impressive white Corinthian pillars adorning the front portico. The house has three levels plus a basement; it contains five fireplaces made with imported Italian tile, six bedrooms and seven bathrooms. Formal entertaining is part of the duties that go along with the commander's position, and this home is well suited for that. The ceilings on the first floor, where the formal dining and reception areas are located, stand over twelve feet high. The general's office was within the house, with a separate entrance. Accompanying the house is a four-car garage, half of which was the original stable for the general's horses. Teddy (when he was a Rough Rider) and Eleanor Roosevelt and John F. Kennedy were guests in this home. Teddy Roosevelt presented a speech from the second-floor balcony, during which he stated that they needed a bigger balcony. Then he looked out to the parade field and explained that they also needed some trees out front. Soon thereafter, a set of trees was planted!

All of our homes hold memories of our families—some good, some bad, but hopefully mostly good. Many paranormal experts theorize that homes and objects can retain energy from the past, and sometimes this residue can replay for us to see. I frequently hear versions of the notorious picture frame story in the top floor of Quarters 92. A large, unattractive picture frame hangs empty on a nail in the third-floor hallway, innocuously enough. It was reportedly left there many families back, hanging in this same spot for centuries. Every time the frame is moved, havoc unfolds, and the original photo subjects that were displayed in the frame make an appearance. A soldier and his large dog materialize, and their spirits noisily romp through the halls. The dog barks, boxes are strewn about, the ceiling fans downstairs spin violently and lights turn on and off. Witnesses, including a police officer, have briefly seen the image of the soldier and the dog as the frame is replaced on the wall. One person described the soldier as wearing a gray uniform and standing in a field of flowers with an Irish setter at his side. Police have been called on more than one occasion when the activity kicks up out of fear that there is an intruder in the home. The commotion ceases when the

Commander's quarters. *Courtesy of Lisa Kindel.*

frame is placed back on the wall. Once the occupants have experienced the antics of the frame, they resist the temptation to touch it again. To forewarn new tenants and visitors, a nameplate has been placed beside the frame that reads, "Ghost of Quarters 92 and Dog." Over the years, the superstition has developed that if the frame is moved, the person who moved it will have bad luck. One painter moved the frame and was fired the next day; another had a heart attack that day. If a person simply touches the frame, he or she is reported to hear incessant dog barking.

When this home was initially built for the brigadier general, four enlisted men were housed in the third-floor attic level. These men were basically his servants, tasked with the upkeep of the house and the general's horses. There is a bedroom on the same floor where a bassinet has been seen rocking on its own. Residents have heard children talking and giggling in the attic when the space is unoccupied. There is other activity within this prestigious home. The front door opens and closes with no human assistance, footsteps resound up and down the old servants' stairwell off the kitchen, disembodied voices echo through the hallways, objects are inexplicably moved and lights turn on and off.

A ghost that the commander's family was used to encountering was upset when the family got transferred recently. Josh, the commander's son, relayed what happened one morning shortly before the move. The family got up and began their daily routine: the kids were dressing for school, and Dad was setting off to work. While the family was preparing for the day, amongst the packing boxes, there was a deafening bang that rumbled throughout the large brick officer's house. All of the doors had simultaneously slammed shut. Enclosed in his bedroom, Josh ran to the door and began tugging on the knob, wanting to escape, but the door would not open. He was locked in his room. All the other members of his family were also confined to the rooms

Quarters 92. *Courtesy of Lisa Kindel.*

they were in. They were all frantically trying to escape their confinement, but eventually the doors just opened. The family was so shaken by the event that it was one o'clock in the afternoon before Josh and his siblings went to school that day.

In 2004, the lady of the house was chatting with trolley guide Val Martin. She said that a couple years earlier, her mother had given her a lovely grandfather clock. To her dismay, the pendulum was lost during their move to WAFB. She purchased a new pendulum, but the clock would not work anymore. Recently, she had been dusting the clock, feeling saddened that it did not work any longer and playing memories of her mother around in her head. At dinnertime, she was discussing the day with her husband when they heard the clock gong. They were happily surprised when they saw that the clock and pendulum were working, and incredibly, it was set at the correct time.

A young carpenter named Brandon was hired to do some finish work out at the base. Working alone inside the decadent general's quarters, Brandon froze when he saw a man in a gray Civil War uniform amble out of the upstairs bathroom and descend the staircase. The soldier's image was very vivid, but it gradually faded as it neared the bottom step.

During the same renovation, Brandon was upstairs when he heard the sound of paper being wadded up. The noise was coming from below on the main floor. Curious, he went down to check it out; he continued to hear the crumpling sound until he reached the living room doorway. All of the paper that he had laid down to protect the flooring had been wadded up into a huge ball and was sitting in the center of the room, with no one around to blame.

Brandon gave his folks a tour of the home while he was working there. He and his parents, Candi and Charlie, were going down the stairs from the top floor when they felt a "tube of cold air" pushing against their backs, forcing them down. They did not feel very welcome at that point.

ALONG OFFICERS' ROW, 94–90

Placed beside the general's quarters on Fort Warren Avenue are several brick Colonial duplex homes, each with its own resident ghost—or at least residual imprints of those who were here from days gone by, holding on to moments in time. Valerie Martin has driven for Cheyenne Street Railway trolleys for more than two decades and has collected many of these stories told here about the officers' quarters.

Officers' Row. *Courtesy of Lisa Kindel.*

Duplex 94 has an art critic spirit that smokes. *Courtesy of Lisa Kindel.*

In Quarters 96A and 96B, a male ghost has been spotted in the basement, and the spirit of a cavalry soldier was observed walking around on the third floor.

Apparently, the ghost inhabiting Quarters 94B is a smoker. While none of the occupants smoke, they often smell the odor of cigar tobacco. The spirit is nonthreatening, but doors have been known to slam with no provocation. The toilet also flushes when no one is in the restroom. Maybe the spirit is considerately flushing his cigar butts?

Moving next door to Quarters 90A, this spirit is an art critic, and the activity here is a bit darker. The resident was an artist. To her dismay, she found her painting smeared over with paint and a knife projecting through the canvas. Her creation was destroyed. Something evil lurks in the shadows of 90A.

DOUBLE TAKE, QUARTERS 90B

When the Cheyenne Street Railway Ghost Tours first began, tour guide Valerie Martin was told that Quarters 90B was the home of a little girl who tragically died in a horseback accident. She was buried in the cemetery beyond the home to the north. If this story is true, it explains some ghostly stories told of 90B from various residents, transpiring several years apart.

The first story is of the family's son, Christopher, waking up during the night. On his way downstairs for a glass of water, he noticed his sister, Lilly, was sleeping in his parents' room, which confused him because he knew that she had spent the night at a friend's house. In the morning, Chris asked his mom why his sister had come home during the night. His mother was so taken aback by the question that she immediately called the friend's house. She was reassured that Lilly was sitting beside her friend at the kitchen table eating breakfast. But Chris insisted that he'd seen a little girl sleeping between his parents.

Valerie Martin told the last account while giving a trolley tour. It so happened that the current residents of 90B were riding the trolley that day. This couple was quite surprised to hear the story because it was so similar to their own experience in 90B. The husband's mother was visiting the family and sharing a bed with her granddaughter in her third-floor bedroom. During the stillness of the night, she got up to use the bathroom. When

A young female spirit resides in Quarters 90. *Courtesy of Lisa Kindel.*

returning to the bedroom, she stopped short at the doorway at the sight of two little girls sleeping in the bed. The additional child had blond ringlets. Nervously, she glanced around the bedroom; looking back at the bed, she found her granddaughter was now alone. The family insisted that Grandma wouldn't lie!

Another previous resident told of hearing an unfamiliar girl's voice saying, "Mommy…Mommy," and then saw the girl's apparition in the hall, visiting from the hereafter. This child feels abandoned in her home on the base, continuously looking for the comfort of her mother.

When one family was preparing to move out of 90B, the packers experienced a door being vigorously shaken, but no one was on the other side. Another family said that on their first night in the home, they heard footsteps echoing throughout the space, step after step thudding against the hardwood floor. As they went to scold their children for being up, they discovered their kids were sound asleep.

A man of the house said he was on the second-floor landing when he heard footsteps and a gurgling noise. At first he assumed it was the humidifier, but when he checked, there was no air rising from the appliance and it was turned off.

SNEAK A PEEK

Brandon, the carpenter I spoke of in the General's Quarters 92, was working at one of the smaller duplexes. Brandon found a little boy from beyond peeking around the corner from the bedroom, watching him work in the upstairs hallway. Brandon spoke to the child but did not get a response. This was not Brandon's first ghostly encounter, so he did not panic. Brandon's interest was piqued by this little guy, so he set out crayons and paper for him but still got no reaction from this young entity. The boy was there for several days, showing himself from another dimension, just hanging out and watching Brandon work.

In another duplex, Brandon could smell a woman's perfume wafting through the living room as if she were right beside him, yet there was no one there.

Brandon became fairly accustomed to these ghostly experiences, but things got a little precarious when one of the spirits actually accompanied him home from the base! He realized what had happened when his television channels started changing randomly whenever he was watching TV. This precocious ghost repeatedly rearranged his knickknacks and possessions in his living room, making his presence known.

FLOATING TOWEL

While I don't know the number of the building where the next story transpired, it's one of the brick officers' quarters. Candace, a major's wife, got up in the middle of the night and quietly crept into the master bathroom. She flipped the light on, and there, in the middle of the bathroom, was a towel floating horizontally in midair. Shocked and mesmerized by what she saw, Candace stood there, her eyes wide with fear. After a moment, she frantically ran out, not worried about being quiet any longer. When she felt brave enough to return to the bathroom, she saw the towel lying in a heap on the floor.

Side by Side, Quarters 82A and 82B

Quarters 82A had been vacant, so the people in number 80 stored some of their belongings in 82A's garage. When new residents were assigned to the empty duplex, they cleaned their stuff out of the garage for the new tenants. The following day, they heard a knock at 82A's door. The new neighbors were standing at their doorstep requesting that they move their items out of their garage. Confused, the people at 82A said that had been done the previous day. They joined their new neighbors in the garage to discover that it was full of their things. Astonished and embarrassed, they moved all of their things out of the garage—again!

In 82B, a baby is heard crying along with a rattle sound. However, no baby resides in the home, and the sounds were not heard from next door.

Cheating Heart (Gus), Quarters 80

The brick corner house is Quarters 80, a single-family field grade officer's home. Val the trolley guide refers to it as Gus's Quarters as she tells this story she heard. When the fort was still quite new, the resident officer came home unexpectedly only to find another fellow, Gus, being kind enough to entertain his wife in his absence. Gus, the enlisted man, tried to escape from the officer through the second-story bedroom window. Completely flustered, he slipped and fell, hanging himself—buck naked, I might add—on the clothesline. It is said to be Gus's spirit that wanders through this home, opening cupboards, moving objects and even rearranging entire rooms of furniture. Val suggested that Gus is simply looking for his trousers!

In 1999, a family living there told Val that they had all seen Gus. Several years later, Val and another driver met a new resident of the home at a military spouses' group Halloween event. The woman discretely told Val that she, too, had seen Gus. One afternoon, she opened the closet door in her master bedroom, and there he was, the spirit of a tall, thin young man with tight red curls and a sheepish grin on his face. At this point, they had to ask her if Gus had his trousers on! She'd been so surprised that she'd slammed the closet door. With great trepidation, she cautiously reopened the door, but Gus was gone. She did say he was wearing a military jacket.

Note: over the years, I've heard a variation of this story, where the couple rendezvoused in Gus's home rather than his mistress's, and when Gus's wife came home, he tried to avoid being caught in his deception by going out the window, at which point he plunged to his untimely death.

One night, Darin, a man living in Quarters 80, went downstairs to find the light on in his office. Curious, he walked into the room, where he clearly saw a man in vintage military attire seated at his desk. This was quite disconcerting. It was his home, his office, his domain—yet there was a strange man who seemed quite comfortable in Darin's chair. Darin took a second to process what he was seeing; clearly, this fellow was not a solid man. It was then that the apparition of the officer dissipated as Darin watched in wonderment. Evidently, the officer had some unfinished business to attend to.

Similar to Quarters 90, a lady in Quarters 80 had her painting studio on the third floor. Frequently, her paints would be smeared together, and her works would be destroyed. Creative people use their skills to express themselves, putting their emotions down on paper. Finding her artwork ruined by an unknown entity was disheartening. She was forced into moving the studio downstairs. Fortunately, the destruction ceased. The spirit was obviously territorial over his third-floor space and wanted her out of there.

In 2006, a colonel told us that her friend lived in Quarters 80 and often spoke of the ghost that inhabits the home, having daily encounters. She said that it blows on her neck. Gus must be up to his old tricks.

Just Around the Bend

Fort Warren Avenue is a very unusually shaped road that resembles a dragon's tail with three zigzag sections. There is a small triangular grassy area referred to as Trophy Park at the first bend. Displayed here is a flagpole, a seven-foot-long Queen Mary Tudor cannon created in the year 1557 and the Bells of Balangiga, which are war trophies acquired during the Spanish-

Bells of Balangiga. *Courtesy of Lisa Kindle.*

American War, when American troops fought in Manila. The attractive quarters continue around the second elbow of Fort Warren Avenue on the north side of the street. The theater and gym are located inside of the bend, and on the south side of the street is the Saint Mithiel Parade Field.

The Brady Bunch, Quarters 78A and 78B

Here's the story of a lovely lady who lived in duplex 78A with her husband, their six children and three spirits. Not exactly the Brady Bunch, but I'll refer to them as Carol and Mike anyway.

There's the stalwart military officer who gives the family the sense that he is commanding and strong yet benevolent. The seventeen-year-old daughter, Marcia, cowered when she heard the imposing male voice speaking directly above her face as she lay in bed. She hid under her covers, eyes scrunched closed and scared out of her wits. Three-year-old Bobby also saw the officer regularly and spoke nonchalantly about the man who inhabited their home.

Mike and Carol had repeated problems with the boiler in the home. The maintenance men were ready to give up in frustration, having found nothing wrong, but then it was as if someone just turned the boiler back on, and everything worked like new. It occurred to them that their male spirit was quite handy around the house. Either that or he was behind the disturbance. This officer was most often seen in the basement.

Then there was a sorrowful wispy woman who wore black and appeared to be in mourning. She had an aura of sadness about her—a heavy sense of despair. The woman was seen only in the dim shadows, usually on the second-floor landing of the servants' stairs, gazing longingly up toward the third floor. She was yearning for her child, the third spirit residing in Building 78A. A young girl of about five years old was primarily seen playing in the unfinished third floor. They described her as mischievous. She liked to play pranks, rearranging the kitchen cupboards and slamming doors. She would often turn on the shower radio so that they would have to run up the stairs and turn it off, but the music would stop just before they reached it. Eventually, they wised up and quit going up to turn it off.

Later, another family moved into Building 78A. A young resident was standing, looking out of a window, when she was firmly pushed from behind. She turned and yelled at her brother, but no one was there. Her brother was not in the room.

Quarters 78, where three spirits reside. *Courtesy of Lisa Kindle.*

As the couple, Ted and Alice, were sprawled out in their bed asleep, a disturbance woke them. They heard people arguing, and as they stirred awake, they both saw the spirits of a man and a woman standing on each side of their bed. Alice nudged Ted; he told his wife, "Let's not get in the middle of this!" The ghostly couple was overheard in many other conversations during the family's occupancy here.

The family decorated for Christmas, displaying their nativity set on top of the television. As the family relaxed and watched holiday programs together, the baby Jesus sprung right off of the television!

Building 78B, the adjoining duplex, also has a ghost. The home was vacant, and a cleaning lady was working on the old servants' stairs. She kept feeling something she couldn't see. It was tickling her neck and back like a feather. Shrugging her shoulders to rid herself of the annoyance, she lost her patience and cussed out loud. She was then pushed down the stairs!

THE COLONEL IN THE STUDY WITH THE CANDLESTICK, QUARTERS 73

Quarters 73 is a substantial, three-story home with a basement that features nine bedrooms and three fireplaces. It's no wonder a spirit would choose to stay on in such a lovely home. In 2003, a colonel's wife who lived here told us that she did not believe in ghosts until living in this home—a sentiment often voiced by base residents. While they hadn't seen the ghost, they often heard him walking on the stairs and heard the creak of opening and closing doors—doors that were actually locked. This ghost had a pungent odor that they struggled to describe. Whenever the smell lingered, the family dogs would intently watch the spot where the odor originated. The dogs would even wake from slumber when the smell occurred. They would jump up, running and barking toward the scent, which was often detected on the stairs.

During the Cheyenne Frontier Days rodeo celebration, the colonel and his wife had company visiting them throughout the festival. There was a cradle set up in the spare room for their infant guest. The baby had been napping. When her parents went in to check on her, they found the cradle swiftly swaying back and forth, as though someone were gently pushing it. This caused them great trepidation. They did not leave their child unattended for a second during the remainder of their visit.

Later, in April 2008, new occupants spoke to Cheyenne Paranormal Investigations (CPI), reporting banging noises from the back of the house, doors opening of their own accord—especially their front door—and noises on the stairwell, along with a strange odor that they likened to wet wool. They said the servants' stairwell by the kitchen was an active area. Footsteps were frequently heard walking up and down that staircase. It's interesting to note that the attics were not finished for the servants. Servants would place their beds beside the fireplace to stay warm. If the homes have finished bedrooms in the attic, they were completed for families with several children.

CPI was invited in to investigate Quarters 73, where it captured disembodied footsteps clamoring overhead, slamming doors below and various other strange noises on tape. The lieutenant assigned to accompany the team became frightened by the distinct footsteps heard overhead during the investigation.

CPI experienced and documented the indescribable odor and the concentrated cold air pockets, particularly by the third-floor landing of the servants' staircase, saying it encompassed a three-foot area. The team encountered the odor on the staircase near the first floor and by the restroom and again on the third floor. While setting up their infrared cameras on the second floor, Scott reached up to pull down the blinds. When he heard a noise behind him, he quickly turned around. Scott and Bob, another team member, clearly saw the CD player deck open on its own. Next, the team heard a little girl singing by the third-floor servants' stairwell. The melody had a definite rhythm to it, but they couldn't name the tune. Moments later, the associated video shows an orb (a light speck or light ball) float directly into Scott's arm. Scott didn't see the light, but he can be heard asking, "Is that you?" in reaction. Throughout the investigation, the team asks, "Is anyone here?" Within moments of asking, the two-way radios squelched, but no one was on the other end. This was immediately followed by two different team members' cellphones vibrating. Again, no one was there when they went to answer. Both Bob's and Scott's new camera batteries were completely drained shortly after entering the home. The batteries from Scott's camera were extremely hot to the touch. It is believed that spirits drain energy, which helps them manifest. CPI felt that paranormal activity within Quarters 73 was substantiated.

Middle Ground, Quarters 72 and 70B

Centrally located, Quarters 72 housed a family who had recently welcomed a new baby into their lives. Mother and baby were often up in the middle of the night. While nursing their child, she would detect the unexplained aroma of pipe smoke in the air surrounding them. Sam, the guard dog, would often react to the anomalies from beyond. A brochure from Fort Russell Days, an annual event on the base, states that the attic originally housed several servants, and the basement held several horses.

As in Quarters 73, a repugnant smell is noticed in an upper-floor bedroom of Quarters 70B, and the door latches are heard clicking open and closed with no mortal assistance, making the residents uneasy.

Misery Loves Company, Quarters 68B

We were told of a nine-year-old girl who died of diphtheria in Building 68B. Now she is seen miserably wondering through the home looking for her mother. The child's footsteps are heard ascending the stairs. Many generations later, teenage girls lived in the home. One day, they curiously followed the spirit up the stairs to the third floor. The girls hysterically ran back down the steps, cold as ice to the touch and extremely frightened. They refused to speak of the experience. It's unusual for teenage girls not to speak. Most encounters with this little girl spirit are not so scary.

BLOODY MAN, QUARTERS 66A AND 66B

There is a straight stretch on Fort Warren Avenue across from Vesle Parade Field that is lined with more stately brick duplexes. Originally, a commanding officer would live on one side with his two lieutenants on the opposite side in these duplexes. In the year 2000, a colonel and his wife lived in 66A. They were good enough to share some of their personal experiences from the house with trolley guide Valerie Martin. The couple said that they had heard about a ghost there before moving in and were a bit concerned because they had an infant to protect. Once they had moved into the home, the couple actually spoke aloud to the spirit inhabitants, saying that they were welcome to stay on the third floor but asked that they please keep away from the baby. The family did face a woman and a young girl from the spirit world regularly, but they coexisted well. They said the little girl would lock the door to the unfinished room in the attic, and they would hear her knocking from the inside.

The following year, new residents said their toddler sometimes saw a "bloody man." How terrifying for this child and his parents. Ten years later, we were told that a cross was turned upside down every single morning. The address is 66, not 666!

In 66B, the adjoining side of the duplex, the name Camille was written on a chalkboard in the attic. No one knew how the name got there or who Camille might have been.

PROTECTOR, QUARTERS 64A AND 64B

In 2009, I had a long, captivating interview with Norma, a former occupant of Quarters 64A. She was very forthright, saying that the family repeatedly saw a male apparition. Describing him in great detail, she said that he had a dark complexion with dark hair and eyes and that he was extremely good looking. He was stocky—standing around five feet, eight inches tall—and was always wearing a green-and-black plaid shirt. The first time they saw him was in the fall of 2002.

Often times, the family members would hear a sound against the house, as if someone were moving a ladder around. They would go outside and walk the perimeter, but there was never anyone there. They would frequently hear the pulling swish of the refrigerator door opening and the popping sounds of a soda can being cracked open. Sometimes they would think it was their older daughter but then would discover that it wasn't her.

There was a big blizzard in March 2003. Windows that had been painted shut for years suddenly opened on their own. The family then smelled something unusual, so they called for assistance. They learned that they had a major gas leak. Had the windows not opened, they most likely would have perished. On a beautiful spring day a month later, Norma tried to pry open the window, but to her dismay, it was sealed by paint. This was one of the windows that had opened the previous month. Norma had to cut through the layers of paint to get the window open.

For Christmas 2003, Norma was given the scary movie *The Others*. After retiring for the evening, she was awakened by loud screams. She got up and soon realized that the movie was blaring and the downstairs lights were on. As she descended the stairs, the movie and the downstairs lights abruptly turned off. The upper hall light remained on. She found herself looking directly into the eyes of the mysterious dark-haired man with the green shirt. She could see him as clearly as she could see any mortal person. She explained that she felt a "warm, inviting sunshine feeling." It was not scary but inviting. He nicely said to her, "We need to learn to live together." She smiled at him and then went back to her bedroom.

This spirit man seemed to be protective of Norma. She was in a heated argument with her husband, "Hal." The quarrel escalated, and the enraged Hal raised his fist toward her. Hal's hand was stopped midair; the man in the green shirt was holding his fist back. Caught completely off guard, Hal screamed out, "Let go of me!" Norma stepped back, and the challenging spirit relinquished his grip. The couple was too astounded to resume their argument.

Norma baked a batch of chocolate chip cookies and a batch of peanut butter cookies. The peanut butter cookies were Hal's favorite. They were arranged on plates on the kitchen counter. When Hal went downstairs in the morning, he was upset to find the peanut butter cookies smashed all over the dining room table. The chocolate chip cookies remained intact on the plate in the kitchen.

The protective man was not their only spirit inhabitant. Their daughters would sometimes see the nonthreatening spirit of a small girl. Norma said that occasionally, while they were in bed, she would feel a cat jump onto their bed. They did not own any pets because one of the girls was allergic. She could feel the cat walk down the center of the bed between her and Hal. The cat smelled awful, but it made her laugh. He always lay on her husband's pillow. She could hear him purring. Sometimes after mopping, she would see dirty paw prints on the floor.

One night while sleeping, they heard a thunderous *Bang!* When they sat up, they were flabbergasted to see the apparitions of a family standing in their master bedroom. The father was in a bluish gray uniform with a flat-topped hat. He was holding a young girl. The wife was in a long skirt, and beside her stood a young boy around nine years old. Hal screamed, "Get out!" with his heart rate quickening. The spirit family obeyed his order. They soon vanished. Hal and Norma got up with weak knees to look for the source of the noise. The couple realized that the cross that hung over the mantle of their bedroom fireplace was now outside of their room. It had moved down the hallway about twenty feet and was just inside another bedroom, lying on floor. There was an indentation on the wall above the fireplace of the cross. Norma took a photograph of the indent. The photo proved to be a token of her sanity, for a few days later, the indent vanished.

The attached duplex, 64B, also has activity. A decade earlier, some trolley riders told us that the young daughter of the family who lived in 64B pointed out an old army uniform when she saw one on display somewhere. She was excited, saying that was what the captain wears. Her parents were confused. "What captain?" they questioned. She replied, "You know, the captain," explaining that he lived in their house. One day, the family watched their daughter tumble downstairs. Before they could get to her, they saw that she was stopped as though someone caught her, and she was set upright.

Other incidents in 64B refer to a young boy spirit that plays with a ball in the attic. Before the ball reaches the opposite wall, it stops and rolls directly back to the little boy. People also say there is most definitely something evil lurking in the coal room at 64B.

WINDOW TO THE SOUL, QUARTERS 60B

In June 2001, trolley driver Valerie Martin interviewed a couple and their two sons. This family lived in Quarters 60B. Upon returning from a camping trip, their neighbor approached them and asked if they had visitors in their absence. The neighbor went on to explain that he had been sitting in his kitchen, drinking coffee, when he looked up to see a little girl with long, curly hair looking out the window while the family was away. The room where the little girl was seen had been a storeroom, but recently, they had fixed up the space as a guestroom. Previously, they had kept the room closed, but after her sighting, the door was continually opening. Between eleven o'clock at night and three o'clock in the morning, the family dog, Abby, would whimper and shake when the door opened. They thought they would just leave the door ajar but discovered it would not stay open. At times, Abby would react from the bedroom, jumping up on the bed and frantically running all around it. Over Memorial Day weekend, an eight-year-old was staying with the family. They put her in the guest bedroom. During the night, she became so frightened that it took them two hours to calm her down.

ROCK-A-BYE BABY, QUARTERS 58

Claire would wake up nearly every night about three o'clock in the morning at Quarters 58. Through the glow of the nightlight, she would see a woman with long, wavy hair standing in the corner swaying back and forth, as though she were comforting a baby—an unbreakable bond. The master bedroom of Quarters 58 has a connecting bathroom that used to be nursery. Claire found the woman enthralling and would just watch her quietly. She asked her husband if he had ever seen the woman, but he thought she was crazy.

ROCKING HORSE, QUARTERS 56B

Before Quarters 58 was ready for a new family to move in, Claire's family temporarily lived next door in 56B. She'd heard that some of the homes on the base were haunted, but she didn't put much stock in the stories. The family immediately noticed that their dogs didn't like the back of the house, and they raised their hackles when going into the attic.

Claire was surprised when her ten-year-old daughter, Morgan, interrupted their company, anxiously telling her that she'd seen a boy in the house. Claire was embarrassed to have her company witness this until she realized just how shaken Morgan was. Claire said Morgan was "as white as a ghost." Her young daughter had been in her playroom on the second floor when she noticed a little boy riding on her rocking horse. Morgan said the boy was dressed weird and went on to describe Victorian clothing—a large sailor collar on his shirt, knickers, buttoned high-top shoes and a beret atop his head. Morgan was not familiar with this style of clothing from so many years ago. She said the boy had glowing green eyes that stared straight ahead the entire time he was riding her rocking horse.

Claire and her husband once saw the spirit of an older man with gray hair and beard. He was standing in a bedroom, attired in an old, grayish wool uniform. He intently stared at them with an evil look but disappeared when the lights were turned on. They never saw him again.

Val was giving a tour to a class of third grade students. During the tour, the teacher told Val that she had lived in Building 56B a decade earlier. She recounted the time when she was doing laundry in the basement. She felt a strong urge to look up, and when she did, she saw a hazy "swoosh," further describing it as a misty, eighteen-inch circular entity whirling around in front of her. The teacher had no logical explanation for her experience. It was something she would never forget.

Staff Circle

North of the charming little white chapel on Fort Warren Avenue is a round street called Staff Circle. The homes were built on a round street in order to keep all the officers from the medical corps together. A runner could quickly beckon all the officers in an emergency so they could dispatch to the hospital, which was located directly behind Staff Circle. The medical corps was not developed until 1889. Before that, soldiers who were being punished would be assigned hospital duty.

Saving Grace, Quarters 48

We've heard a lot about a fun-loving ghost, dubbed Jack, that lives in Quarters 48A. I believe spirits have the same personality in the next, higher dimension that they had here on earth—other than the fact that they may be more enlightened. Jack is a very social ghost, surrounding himself with spirits and libations. Jack is often heard walking the halls at two o'clock in the morning. The footsteps subside at the back door.

Amber lived in Building 48A and was awakened night after night for two weeks straight one summer by a raucous party inside her home. One of these nights, she heard the thunderous crash of her china cabinet slamming over and all the china breaking. Totally disheartened, she remained in bed. When she inspected her home in the morning she was thrilled to find her cabinet and dishes intact.

Matt, a former trolley driver, spoke to a major who lived in Building 48A for several years. The major said his mother, "Grace," recuperated there after open-heart surgery and had many interactions with the boisterous Jack during her stay. Grace was in the habit of falling asleep with the television turned on. She kept waking up to silence and asked the family not to turn the TV off, but they all said they had not done so. Realizing it was their friendly spirit, Grace told Jack that she knew he was trying to help, but would he please leave the television on. The television never turned off during the night after that.

One day, Grace slipped at the top of the stairs. She tumbled down the first flight, and bouncing past the landing, she continued falling down the second flight of stairs. On the second landing, Grace felt invisible hands on her shoulders stop her. They gently pushed her back onto the landing, keeping her from descending the third set of stairs. Grace was so grateful that Jack had saved her from further harm. While battered from the fall, she did heal in time.

Various occupants of Quarters 48B have said that Jack occasionally visits them and the five-year-old boy spirit that resides there. The boy is seen and heard tromping around in the attic in his cowboy boots.

Father of the Air Force, Quarters 47

Quarters 47 was home to Captain Billy Mitchell, who was known as the father of the air force in 1912. He was a visionary of the air force and its possibilities. He persistently made his opinions heard and was eventually acknowledged for his efforts.

In 1994, the kitchen was remodeled in Quarters 47. The occupants began experiencing an unfamiliar smell. It was not a bad odor but rather a masculine smell, perhaps imprinted here by the captain. Often times, renovations to a home will stir up the spirits.

TEA PARTY, QUARTERS 46

The new tenants in Quarters 46 had moved in that week and were in the tedious process of unpacking. Meredith had laid out her china on the dining room table but had not placed it in the cabinet yet. Running out of steam, she retired for the night. She woke up to the sounds of her china clinking. She immediately thought that her cat was walking across the table disturbing the dishes. Then she realized that her cat was still in quarantine from the move. Was this the spirit of a cat walking across the table, or was she hearing a ghostly tea party?

TOM, DICK AND HARRY, QUARTERS 44

In 2009, a new nurses' day room was opened in Quarters 44. We have a story from this building about a cleaning lady who was terrified by the barking of a large dog that could not be seen with the naked eye. She left the home, refused to be alone in the building and brought reinforcements back with her so she could finish her duties.

In 2008, before the space was converted to the nurses' day room, three buddies were staying there for a week. I'll call them Tom, Dick and Harry. They shared an apartment with a common living space. Tom was a retired navy man with fifteen years under his belt. He was continually tripping over a trash can next to the television in his room. The thing is, that trash can belonged in another area of the apartment, but it kept turning up next to his television with the lid off and turned upside down. Dick woke up night after night with the television in his room blaring. He had turned the television off before going to sleep. He started sleeping on the sofa in the living room. Harry became really frightened in Quarters 44 and asked to be transferred to another lodging location. He refused to speak of his encounters.

LIVE IN HARMONY, QUARTERS 42

Folks in Building 42B are sometimes spooked by their high-strung ghost that knocks things off the nightstands and wildly moves the window shades up and down. Sometimes, the blinds actually fall out of the window frame. Most often, this occurs in the dark of night. The light bulbs break inside the lamp, suggesting that the spirit is feeding off the energy from the lamp. On another note, this spirit often winds the music box, listening to its calming, melodious tune.

PARADISE, QUARTERS 40

One theme that seems consistent throughout this post is that the spirits seem to linger in the attics. Quarters 40 is no different. Many years ago, a resident said that her daughter liked to sleep in the attic with the ghost. Longing for a tropical paradise, the 2004 occupants got creative and set up a tiki bar in the attic. They said they had a lot of unusual things happen up there. The husband chuckled, saying that sometimes when he came home from work, he would go up there and hear his wife greet him. He would respond and then realize she was not there. She had not returned home from work. At least the spirit is cordial and enjoys their little slice of paradise.

TRAVELING SALESMAN, QUARTERS 30

In 1906, Secretary of War William Taft recommended that Fort Russell be expanded to a brigade-sized post. Quarters 30 was one of the new two-story brick quarters that went up during that expansion. The home is one of only fifteen field grade officers' quarters on the base that is not a duplex. Two sisters who lived there relayed that they saw the apparition of a man in a blue suit on the third floor of their home. They said he reminded them of a traveling salesman!

DOLLHOUSES, QUARTERS 28, 27, 24 AND 22

When the post was made a permanent installation in 1885, substantial redbrick homes were constructed there, replacing the original wooden barracks that were slapped up as temporary housing. The charming brick homes were built as officers' quarters. Later, they were nicknamed the "dollhouses" because when the newer homes were built, they were much larger than these. The dollhouses' historic value is part of the reason the base has been designated as a national landmark. The dollhouses are some of the oldest structures on the base that are still in use today.

The nine brick dollhouses were built with staircases in the back of the home connecting the kitchen to the top floor so the servants could go to their quarters without walking through the house and disturbing the family. Seven of the dollhouses still exist today. Each of the dollhouses includes a formal parlor and dining room, along with a family room, three bedrooms and a porch on the back. They all have an additional servant's room on the second floor.

Virginia, a woman who lived in one of the enchanting dollhouses as a child, remembers there was a bathroom just off the second-floor landing. One night, she went to use the restroom and encountered the ethereal apparition of a radiant lady in a flowing blue gown standing on the landing. The curious young girl spoke to the woman, but she dissipated before the child's eyes. Virginia vividly remembers the woman in blue to this day.

Dollhouse 28 is now assigned to those who neither have nor want cats, as many felines have died here in unexplained, gruesome ways over the years. In Dollhouse 27, the lights turn on by themselves in the middle of the night. People living in Dollhouse 24 tell of unexplained clanging noises. A family said their five-year-old boy complained of a male spirit that wanted to play with him, but the boy said he was too rough. It was uncomfortable for the boy. Residents at Dollhouse 22 are sometimes rudely shaken awake by an unseen spirit.

RENDEZVOUS WITH A GHOST, QUARTERS 21

Building 21 sits among the dollhouses but is larger and has been renovated for visitors. Guests frequently say that they are rudely shaken awake by an entity. In 2004, people staying here said they heard the floor creaking as it does when someone walks across it, but no one was seen there. They also heard doors shutting on their own.

The next year, Kelli and Jim were temporarily staying on the second floor. Kelli was taking a catnap. She was awakened at 3:28 p.m. by a lingering kiss. While still in a state of slumber, she thought Jim had returned from work but was very disturbed when reality crept in and she realized no one there. She had felt the sensation of a presence and the pressure of two invisible fingers against her cheek. It is quite fortunate that the spirit drew the line with a kiss and was not a more lurid incubus.

A housekeeper was cleaning the restroom of room seven when the door suddenly closed behind her. She heard the door close and turned around to see why. At first, she thought a co-worker must have closed it, but no one replied to her inquiry. Turning the knob and pulling strongly on the door, she realized she was locked in the confined space. Getting nervous, she called out for help. The staff heard her; they had to take the door off its hinges from the outside to let her out. She was locked in for about fifteen minutes. The poor lady was so scared that she was trembling as they escorted her out.

ORIGINAL FORT D.A. RUSSELL: DIAMOND IN THE ROUGH

The farthest west bend of Fort Warren Avenue is where the original Fort D.A. Russell was established in 1867. The barracks and miscellaneous buildings were laid out in the shape of a diamond to minimize the effects of the strong prairie winds. There were no trees to help block the winds at that time. The officers' quarters were not completed until the enlisted men's barracks were done.

The commanding officers' quarters were built at the northern point of the diamond, and the guardhouse (jail) was placed opposite on the southern point. The grassy area inside of the diamond was the original parade field. It is now called Marne Parade Field. This has been the site of numerous parades and sporting events over the past century and a half. The fort was designed to accommodate twelve companies—six cavalry and six infantry. The seven double infantry officers' barracks were built on the northwest side, with the infantry soldiers' barracks on the southwest side. The officers' quarters were split, with the captain living on one side and his two lieutenants on the other side. The seven double cavalry officers' barracks were on the northeast side, and the

cavalry soldiers' were on the southeast side of the diamond. The main difference between cavalry and infantry is that the cavalry rode in and fought on horseback or mules while the infantry were foot soldiers—they went into battle and fought on foot. The cavalry were considered the elite, even though the infantry won more battles and killed more Native Americans. The humble buildings were constructed with planed boards with a mud mixture filling the cracks. They were quite cold and drafty but much better than the tents the men had lived in during their first four months on the garrison.

The officers were allowed to have chickens and cows behind their quarters. Many animals ran loose around the post. There are articles that mention the many annoying goats. They also planted gardens; they wouldn't get much fresh food otherwise. The soldiers' barracks did not have indoor plumbing for the first fourteen years, but in 1881, they got both plumbing and electric lights.

Officers' Row, 1868 Fort D.A. Russell. *Courtesy of WY State Archives.*

Most of the other required buildings—a hospital, warehouses, blacksmith and carpenter shops and a bakery—were placed just east of this diamond. A school was never built on the fort. The children gathered in any building that had space. They were taught the basics by enlisted men, who were paid extra for this service. Even today, the base children attend school just outside the base's perimeter. The original post was not large at all; however, the fort eventually became the largest cavalry post in the United States. There was no stockade build around the fort. Now a fence lines the perimeter of the base.

One of the cavalry second lieutenant's wives died shortly after arriving. She was diagnosed with dysentery. Her system was severely weakened, and she then developed pneumonia, which proved fatal. She may be one of the female spirits regularly seen in this oldest section of the base.

By the 1870s, social happenings at the fort were top notch. Many of Cheyenne's upper crust would climb into their carriages and traverse the three miles to hear the military band play in the old post hall.

Today, the last section of Fort Warren Avenue is the north side of the original diamond-shaped fort. The simple wooden barracks along the southeast side of the diamond were torn down when the base was designated a permanent installation. New brick barracks went up just a bit south and to the east of the torn-down wooden buildings, along what is today known as Randall Avenue. The first brick infantry barracks were converted into a salvage warehouse in 1926.

Fort Russell Commander's Residence, Quarters 8

In 1903, the elaborate Quarters 8 was built on the north point of the diamond to be the commanding officer's home. It was bigger than the existing dollhouses and was considered a mansion with over five thousand square feet of living space. The built-in courting bench still sits in the front yard, and the original copper sink remains in the home.

A previous colonel who lived there with his family told a security forces man we interviewed that they would hear kids playing all the time.

Quarters 7 and 8, once the commanding officer's home. *Courtesy of Jill Pope.*

Sometimes, it was in the middle of the night. He would get up to scold his children, only to find them tucked into their beds and sawing logs. He spoke out loud to the spirit kids and said that they needed to be quiet during the night and let his children sleep. He was pleased to say that they quit making noises after his children went to bed.

FIREWALKER (WHERE QUARTERS 7 IS NOW)

In the early days of the fort, the only way to extinguish fires was with a bucket brigade. Fires were a huge problem in Cheyenne. Once a spark was struck, the prairie winds would catch hold, and the dry prairie grasses and wooden buildings would go up in an instant. There was not an abundance of water while the town and fort were being built along Crow Creek.

It was the heart of winter—fifteen degrees below zero at four o'clock in the morning on January 4, 1875—when Lieutenant Pardee's quarters were discovered in flames. The water barrels were frozen solid. Soldiers rushed in and tried to salvage some belongings before everything was lost. The blaze caught life from the strong winds. Six sets of quarters on the west side of the parade field were destroyed. The fire had started from an overheated stovepipe. Despite the heat from the fire, many of the men got frostbite on their hands and feet.

Private Henry Myers, Company L, Third Cavalry, was killed while recovering the possessions of Lieutenant Pardee. He is buried at the base cemetery in plot B49. The official records state "burned to death." Private Myers is still seen roaming the area where the fire occurred. Those quarters were not replaced, but after the turn of the century, Quarters 7 was built there.

WATERPROOF, PERSHING HOUSE, QUARTERS 2

Quarters 2 is not considered a dollhouse because it is considerably larger. It was built in 1885 as the commanding officer's home and was the largest home on the post at the time, containing nine fireplaces and an inviting southern-style front porch. In 1903, Quarters 8 was built next door. It was bigger and more elaborate than Quarters 2, so it then became the commanding officer's home.

Later, in 1912, Quarters 2 was assigned to Captain John "Blackjack" Pershing. Young Frankie Warren fell in love with Pershing, the dashing army captain who attended West Point. Her powerful father, Senator Francis E. Warren, was not elated that his daughter was going to marry a common captain. While he liked Pershing, he was worried a captain would not be able to keep her in the manner to which she was accustomed. Having friends in high places, Warren called in a favor. In 1905, the couple was married; six months later, Captain Pershing became General Pershing, ahead of 862 senior officers, at the hands of Warren's hunting buddy, President Teddy Roosevelt. Pershing did prove himself worthy, however. He commanded the United States forces in World War I. After the war, he was promoted to general of the armies. The only other man ever to hold this title was none other than George Washington. There have been sightings of Pershing himself on the parade field in front of his former home, Quarters 2.

Soon thereafter, Pershing was stationed at the Presidio in California. In August 1915, while General Pershing was away on duty, Frankie and their three daughters and son were in the Presidio home when a devastating fire erupted after hot coals fell onto the heavily waxed floor. There was not enough water to put the fire out, and all four women perished, leaving only young Warren—age five—behind with his father. Frankie was a Cheyenne native. The family is buried in Cheyenne's Lakeview Cemetery.

The energy from Blackjack's grief and this horrific event have imprinted on Quarters 2 as the ghosts that reside there and oversee and protect the occupants, making certain that there is always plenty of water on hand.

Blackjack Pershing's residence, Quarters 2. *Courtesy of Jill Pope.*

Preparing for a dinner party, Andrea, the hostess, pre-set the table. She filled a water pitcher and set it in the dining room shortly before the guests were to arrive. When she returned to the room to fill the glasses, she discovered the glasses were already full with the ice water from the pitcher. She stood there staring at the glasses for some time. After regaining her composure, Andrea went on with her party preparations. When she returned to the dining room, she found that the water pitcher had also been refilled.

Another day, a candle was unintentionally left burning in the house. The occupants found water pooled around the candlewick upon their return. The protective ghost had extinguished the candle for them.

Occupants of Quarters 2 have heard the washing machine running in the middle of the night when no one is up. The toilets are also heard flushing when no one is in the restroom. Other residents report that they have gone away on vacation and come back to find that all of the houseplants have been watered for them. Most of the unexplained stories we are told from Quarters 2 have water themes, but there are also a few reports of windows slamming shut in the night, disembodied footsteps treading across the second floor, doors banging closed and pictures plummeting off the wall.

Shirley, a woman we met, said they were visiting the family who lived in Quarters 2, with no idea of the peril they were in for. She said that her husband, Robert, was literally thrown out of bed during the night. Shirley explained that he was lying on his side, facing the edge of the bed, when he was thrust onto the floor by a vile, unseen force. Robert landed flat on his back, which seems an unlikely position to land in if he had simply rolled out of bed. There was a distinct red mark across his right cheek, which didn't make sense since he landed on his back. Robert was uncertain of why he was the subject of this entity's fury.

While working on the 2005 trolley ghost tour, driver Valerie Martin and I interviewed the current resident at Quarters 2. She said they witnessed a purple hue glowing in their bedroom that appeared out of nowhere. Their closet door rapidly moves of its accord. Nancy recounted that her husband became so intrigued by the spirit events that were happening in their home that he bought specific computer and electronic equipment to record the white noise. The couple concluded that there are three separate spirits occupying their home. They confidently report that there is an English man, a woman named Eva and a three-year-old boy that is seen running in the living room. They claim to have recordings of the man with the English accent saying his name is Dave Walters. The pair has found documentation of a Private Lawrence D. Walters, buried at the WAFB cemetery in section D, number 343, who died on January 25, 1923. The couple has seen this man's apparition twice, describing him as having curly blond hair. They have captured recordings of a disembodied voice saying, "Steven, up here! Emergency in the bath!" They recorded a male voice with a bleak message, saying, "Men are dying." They also recorded a whistle. I have not heard the audio recordings or seen the documentation, but I am thoroughly intrigued.

Buffalo Soldier, Quarters 1

Quarters 1, built in 1885, is the oldest home on the base and is one of the original nine dollhouses. This home is on the original diamond and not situated in the row with the other dollhouses.

The brochure from the 1995–96 Fort D.A. Russell historic homes tours mentions a ghost called "Willie" here. In 1996, a new family was moving into this lovely home. The father sent his excited daughter, Amelia, upstairs to select her new bedroom. She came sauntering back down with a peculiar look on her face. When questioned, she said she would take Willie's room.

Quarters 1 is the oldest house on the post. *Courtesy of Jill Pope.*

Confused, her father questioned her further. Amelia said a man named Willie had been in the room upstairs, and she watched him float out of the window. Her father flew up the stairs to inspect the room, making sure there was no intruder. From Amelia's description of her new friend, they believe Willie to be a Buffalo Soldier. The Native Americans called the African American men from the Ninth Cavalry Buffalo Soldiers because they thought the unfamiliar men's dark color and curly hair resembled the buffalo. The Ninth Cavalry was one of only four African American army regiments—those were the Ninth and Tenth Cavalries and the Twenty-fourth and Twenty-fifth Infantries. The Ninth Cavalry was stationed at Fort Russell from 1910 to 1912. John Pershing commanded the Ninth Cavalry Buffalo Soldiers; this is where he got the nickname "Blackjack Pershing." Willie proved to be an amicable spirit and cohabited well with the family.

DOUBLE TROUBLE: ECTOPLASM, QUARTERS 20A

There are five historic brick duplexes placed on the row where the original cavalry officers' temporary barracks once stood on the northeast side of the original diamond-shaped fort. These flimsy homes were used for fourteen years. Eighty men lived in each barracks, so there is ample opportunity for spirit activity.

Quarters 20A is one of these five brick duplexes. There is far more than meets the eye going on there. Brandy, the family dog, refused to go in the basement at their duplex, 20A, but she loved romping in the attic. Brandy would exuberantly run around in the attic, bouncing off the walls. Other occupants have said their animals acted similarly. What causes me to pause more than the animals' behavior is the yellow substance that is referred to as ectoplasm—a syrup-like substance associated with ghosts. Ectoplasm is said to be created when an entity tries to manifest itself. Ectoplasm was found streaming across the ceiling and dripping into the tub in this duplex.

The ghost in neighboring Duplex 18B roams in silence. He does like it hot, turning the thermostat up to ninety degrees every day, even in the summer. Maybe he was one of the original fort soldiers who had to endure prairie life in a tent for four months during the blustery cold winter of 1867.

In Building 12A, the ghost opens the refrigerator and the kitchen cupboards (sounds like a teenager). A girl who lived in the home told her parents that she sees a "penguin girl," apparently referring to the spirit's dated clothing. The penguin girl would join the young boys residing there

Ectoplasm was observed in Quarters 20 (right). *Courtesy of Jill Pope.*

when they would play with their train sets in attic. The boys spoke of her freely. Whenever they tried to watch *The Simpsons*, the channel would change (guess she wasn't a fan of the show). They told their parents that the girl and her mother both died of the flu. There were many cases of dysentery, diphtheria, yellow fever and scarlet fever on the post in the 1800s. The boys told their parents, "She's mean today," but went on to explain that it was the anniversary of her death.

In Building 12B, the lady of the home told us her eight-year-old son wasn't comfortable in his attic bedroom. When she asked him why, he said it just didn't feel right in there. Listen to that gut instinct.

In Building 10A, also on northeast side of the Fort Russell diamond, we have reports from two different tenants of the blinds opening or closing "by themselves" back in the 1990s. By the end of the decade, their spirit inhabitants had begun turning the computer on (guess they're keeping up with new technology).

MISCELLANEOUS HOME STORIES

Fire Servant

We have documented a story of the apparition of an African American lady who lovingly tucked live children into their beds at night. She is believed to be the ghost of a servant who rescued children from a fire by tossing them from the second-story window of the home, while she herself perished in the flames. This would be one of the historic homes on Fort Warren Avenue that had servants' quarters.

Attic Man

Craig, one of the Security Forces men, and his wife kindly offered to babysit for another base couple. While cozied in on the couch, they heard noises coming from above, so Craig and King, the family's pit bull, went to investigate. When Craig opened the attic door, he felt a cold breeze rush past him, and King took off running. Feeling leery, Craig peered inside; he didn't see anything that could have caused the noise. As he slowly descended the stairs, he was trying to rationalize what had just happened. Mason, the preschool child they were babysitting, stood wide-eyed at the bottom of the steps. He said, "Did you see the bad man, too?"

Dinner Roulette

Allie, a high school girl, was spending the night with Jaidyn, a friend who lived on base. Jaidyn's father was a squadron commander.

The girls set the dining room table in preparation for dinner. They went into another room briefly, and when they returned, all the place settings had been neatly moved to other places on the large table. They stood there, perplexed, wondering how things got neatly rearranged. After a moment, they went into the kitchen to get the food to be served. When they came back into the dining room, the place settings had been moved to completely different spots again.

Jaidyn told Allie that sometimes the window would open by itself. She said that that if they went to shut the window, the door would open. If they closed the door, the window would open—it was like a game.

Vacant but Occupied

Amanda and Tara were teenage girls who lived on the base. They went for a walk on the western edge of the base, just past the original Fort Warren diamond. There are several old vacant brick duplexes by a huge field. Torn, ragged curtains still hang in windows. It caught Tara's attention when she saw one of the curtains move. Grabbing onto Amanda's arm, she burst out, "Did you see that?" Amanda turned toward the house, and both of the girls saw a huge dark shadow dart across the room in front of the window. At the same time, they heard a thunderous thumping noise. They broke into a fast sprint across the field. Terrified, they continued running all the way home. Normally, I would blame this on a vagrant, but they do not have vagrants milling about on a secure military base.

Ominous Message

Moving past Fort Warren Avenue, there are a couple of streets that run north to south that are lined by newer duplex housing. These streets form the western border of the air force base, with nothing but prairie beyond them within the base confines. The next two stories occurred there.

This account and the following investigation came to me from the esteemed Rocky Mountain Paranormal Research Society (RMPRS) of Denver, Colorado. Refer to the Paranormal Investigation chapter in the beginning of this book for information on this group. The team was called in when the tenants received an ominous message from restless occupants on the other side.

These incidents took place in 2005. RMPRS promised anonymity to the family, so all it would divulge is that it was one of these last two streets on the western side. The team found the family to be well adjusted and did not feel they were being dishonest.

A few months after Sam, Cathy and their eight-year-old son, Brian, moved into a two-story home near FamCamp, they began to experience strange occurrences. Cathy walked downstairs and confronted a clear manifestation of a Native American spirit; his long, oily, black hair was pulled back and thinning at the ends. He wore a T-shirt, and she estimated he was about forty-five years old. He gave her a dreadfully disapproving look with his long, stern face, causing her to run and lock herself in the bathroom. Then she heard a young female's piercing cry while she retreated into the bathroom. Cathy wondered if it was the spirit of the screaming Indian woman that is often heard along the creek in FamCamp.

A month later, when Sam arrived home from work, he saw a dark silhouette in the form of a human standing in his front window. He rushed into the house, but the figure was gone. That's when Sam noticed a smaller, dog-shaped black shadow rapidly scurry down the hall, turn sharply into the kitchen and disappear through the closed and locked back door. Sam and Cathy didn't have any animals. Sam called the security police, and they swept the house from top to bottom for a home intrusion but found nothing.

Two more months passed before young Brian awoke in the night, terrified of a man standing behind a chair in his bedroom. Wearing a modern-style blue work shirt and blue jeans, the white man had gray hair and a long beard. Brian said the man was "kinda smiling and seemed nice." The man walked to the window, where he disappeared. Since then, Brian refuses to be away from his parents' sides when in the house, sleeping in their bedroom and sitting outside the bathroom door when his mom is in there. RMPRS interviewed the boy separately from his parents, and there were no discrepancies in the accounts.

Within the next month, the occurrences worsened. With so many footsteps heard thudding on the staircase, doors and drawers opening and slamming closed in the kitchen during the middle of the night, objects disappearing only to show up in unusual places, candles lighting on their own and isolated cold spots, the family generally stayed together, not even daring to go to the kitchen for a glass of water alone.

One morning, they found a sweet-smelling, reddish-brown smear all over the refrigerator door spelling out the brazen words "go now"—a message left for them by former residents. They intently searched the kitchen for a matching substance, checking all the jellies and sauces. Nothing matched the material on the door.

The family finally brought two dogs home, hoping they would feel more secure. The dogs would stare into thin air and chase invisible things around the bedroom. It was at this time that they called Rocky Mountain Paranormal Research Society for help.

It was a ridiculously windy day in January when the team arrived. This wind made it difficult to discern unusual noises within the home. The group toured the home and did interviews and baseline readings before wiring up their microphones and night-vision cameras. They also interviewed the neighbors, who said that their toilet seat would rise on its own but did not admit to any further activity.

The team found that a closed window in the master bedroom had opened by itself during the investigation. Unusual tapping sounds were recorded in Brian's bedroom, where one of the team members felt quite uneasy. They could not absolutely discount the wind as the cause. Most remarkable was witnessing the couple's bed vibrating.

North Side Homes

We have some stories from some of the newer housing divisions on the post. While these structures are much newer than the historic brick buildings, the entire base overflows with history.

Number 1622B Washakie Loop is on the north side of the base. Sybil's twelve-year-old son called her at work. He was freaked out because he saw a man standing in his parents' bedroom. He turned his head for a closer look, and the man disappeared right in front of him. Sybil went home to check on things, but everything was fine.

Number 1904 Seneca Avenue is also on the north end of the post. The couple living there hears footsteps making their way across the room above them when they are both on the main floor. They hear the clicking and gliding sound of the front door opening, but no one is standing there to greet them.

Peekaboo, Piute Drive

Number 1738 Piute Drive is in the same housing division. From the first day that Gina and Frank lived there, it always felt like someone was watching them. Before moving to WAFB, they hadn't experienced anything paranormal, but unusual things started to happen to them now. Mother and daughter were hanging out in the living room. Sierra was just four months old. She was sitting in her swing while Gina was watching television from the couch across the room. Sierra kept turning toward a corner near the kitchen. She began giggling really hard. Gina could not figure out what she was looking at. Gina would say her name, and then Sierra would turn and look at her mother and stop laughing, but soon she turned her gaze back to the corner and started laughing again. She was fixated on the corner. It seemed like someone was playing peekaboo with her.

One morning, Gina got up before sunrise. She was surprised to see the lights on in the bedroom of her nine-year-old daughter, Julianna. Julianna was sound asleep. Later, Gina asked her why she slept with the lights on, and she said that there was a girl in her room at night. Julianna was able to describe her clothes, height and the look on the child's face in detail. When she came home from school that day, she drew a picture of what she saw, and her parents felt that the drawing looked like a Native American boy. She drew the child wearing pants of two colors and a black jacket with long dark hair. Julianna often relayed to her parents instances of seeing and hearing the ghostly child.

Gina and Julianna were cleaning out Julianna's closet one afternoon. Gina carried some things out of the bedroom while Julianna continued sorting through her things. The closet door was open when Gina left the room. As she walked down the hall, she heard it loudly slam close. When she turned toward the noise, Julianna came running out of her bedroom, fleeing to her mother. Crying, she said the door deliberately slammed closed by itself and scared her. The doors in those old houses were wooden sliding doors and very hard to open and close.

A group of wives began to share their paranormal experiences with one another. Intrigued by all their combined encounters, they decided to do a bit of investigating in their homes. In Gina's home, they captured audio of footsteps on the stairs and video of unidentifiable blue lights. Their flashlights were turning on and off without assistance, and a photograph of the empty house shows something that looks like eyes.

Hitchhikers: Ute Drive

Tammy lived on Ute Drive. She nearly called the police one night because she was so frightened by the escapades of her ghost. Tammy was in her bedroom when she heard heavy boots striding through her house. Then the cabinet doors began slamming. She came to realize that the disturbance was made by an unearthly being.

This spirit made its presence known by opening doors. Tammy was constantly finding closed doors somehow opened. It's a problem when she leaves her house and comes home to find the door wide open.

Her small dog refuses to go to near the basement. They have tried to entice him down with toys and treats but to no avail.

The ladies' group did a bit of investigating in Tammy's home, and the following morning, her fellow investigator Gina found her door ajar. They wondered if the spirit had followed her home.

I found the door incident interesting simply because I have another, almost identical story from a man who lived in one of the duplex officers' quarters behind the hospital. Dave, a passenger on a 2012 trolley tour, said that he had visited a friend on base. As they sat at the kitchen table with their coffee, she told him that she would frequently find her front door wide open. She couldn't figure out how the door was opening. She would always make sure to close it tightly. They talked about the unusual noises heard within the home, and she said that the lights would turn on and off by themselves. Dave went home, and in the morning when he awoke, he found that his door was wide open. He feared that the ghost had traveled home with him.

Things That Go Bump in the Night: 1732A Piute Drive

Rebecca and Mark lived at 1732A Piute Drive. Rebecca would catch a glimpse of her husband and hear him move through their house. She would follow him to engage in a conversation, only to find he was not there. Her husband expressed having the same experience, thinking he saw Rebecca and going to speak to her, but he would discover that he was alone and search all around, wondering just whom he had seen in their house.

They really do have things that go bump in the night in their house. There would be banging noises emanating from the basement. When Rebecca or Mark went down to find the source, the noise would instantly stop and become dead silent.

They could hear someone walking up and down the stairs and stalking the hallway at night, interrupting their sleep. Every time they got up to check, they would not find anything or anyone to explain the sounds. It was quite unnerving.

DORMITORIES

The military began building brick barracks for the soldiers at Fort Russell in 1906. The first floor had individual rooms for officers. The second floor was an open bay—a large common room for a number of men to reside in. Today, many of these barracks have been renovated into several dorm rooms on both floors for the enlisted men and women. It's interesting to note that the barracks' attics were used as firing ranges during World War II.

In 2010, Ron, a Security Forces officer, told me that their well-trained patrol dogs would not go into the attic of a dorm building. They will go as far as the door, but then they get skittish, digging their paws into the floor and refusing to cross the threshold.

Security forces received a call regarding one of the dorms and made a service call. There was a light on in the attic. The serviceman went up and turned the light off. When they were pulling away in their car, Ron looked up and was agitated to see that the light was back on.

One of the dorm buildings built as soldiers' barracks, 1906–10. *Courtesy of Lisa Kindel.*

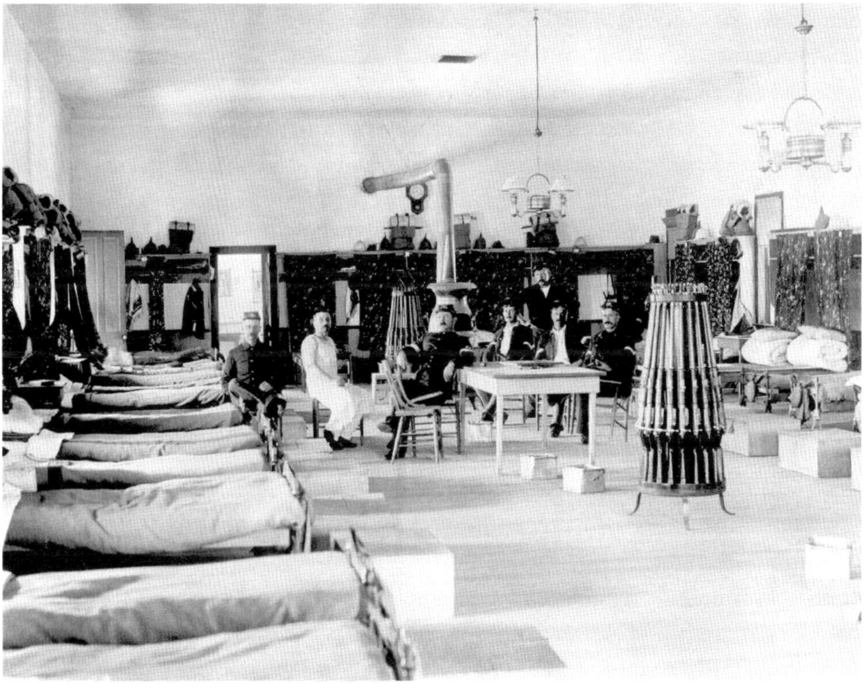

Open barracks. *Courtesy of Wyoming State Archives.*

Horsing Around

In 2007, I met Andrew, a nice young airman who lived in Dorm 224. He and his roommate would often hear horses galloping. The unseen animals were so close that they could hear them breathing and snorting. When they would get up to inspect, there were no horses outside their dorm or anywhere in the vicinity. This happened several times.

"Ring Around the Rosie," Dorm 220

In the 1990s, Allison was a paramedic for the base ambulance service. She told me that on slow evenings, they would sometimes pull into the parking lot at the indoor gym (Building 314). They were sitting there one night, drinking coffee to keep them alert, when they noticed a light shining out of the fourth-floor window of Building 220, the old nurses' dorm that was built in 1909. The building looks distinguished, but in reality, danger lurks here. The light looked like a flashlight pointing outward from the window. The light then traveled the length of the building, going swiftly from one window to the next. They had been inside this building in the past. What struck them as peculiar was the fact that this floor was split into several rooms, and you could not walk the direct line the light was traveling. Knowing that the base has a plethora of ghost stories, they got a bit creeped out. The next day, they spoke to the dorm chief. He asked if they knew the history of this building—they did not. He proceeded to tell them that in the base's early days, Building 220 had served as the nurses' dorms. He said there were two nurses who hanged themselves in the fourth-floor attic. Since then, specters of the nurses have been seen. Even more extraordinarily, occasionally pieces of old rope would be found up there.

One of the most enthralling paranormal events on base happened in Building 220. This account will make your blood run cold. I learned this inexplicable story from Valerie Martin. Val met Paige, a female captain who shared her terrifying experience. Paige was temporarily staying in the airmen's quarters.

In the middle of the night, Paige awoke to the garish sight of five people who were wearing vintage clothing, holding hands and dancing in a circle at the foot of her bed. They eerily chanted the familiar words:

An eerie "Ring Around the Rosie" apparition occurred at Dorm 220. *Courtesy of Lisa Kindle.*

Ring around the rosie…
pocket full of posies…
ashes, ashes, we all fall down.

For a moment, time seemed to stand still. Terrified, Paige pulled the covers over her head, afraid to even breathe. She could hear her own heart's rapid beating.

Finding her nerve, she slowly pulled the covers down. Much to her horror, there was a face floating just above her own. A hand reached out and harshly slapped Paige across the face. Heart racing, she tore out of the room and kept running until she was outside. Petrified, Paige raced next door to billeting, refusing to enter Building 220 ever again. She could not mask her fear. They took her seriously, not only because she was trembling and quite convincing, but also because she had a vivid red handprint across her face. Someone else retrieved her belongings in the morning. What a tantalizing look into the afterlife.

The "Ring Around the Rosie" nursery rhyme has a dark origin, tracing back to the black plague in London. In the 1660s, the streets of London were like the bowels of hell. There were no sanitation standards. The streets were filled with mounds of trash and open sewers. The plague was one of the most devastating pandemics in our world's history. It was very contagious and was spread by rats and fleas. People inflicted with the plague would develop rose-colored sores all over their bodies. The sores had a circle around them—the "ring around the rosie." The inflicted also developed a putrid odor. Many victims carried "posies" of herbs in their pockets to ward off the stench. Some folks also believed that incense and perfume oils would kill the disease. Upon death, the bodies were burned, preventing the spread of the contagious, heinous disease—"ashes, ashes, we all fall down."

When people perished from the plague, their homes were quarantined. The doors were marked with large red crosses. Watchman stood guard for forty days, at which time they believed it was safe to reenter the home. Why the spirits of Building 220 would recite this nursery rhyme to Paige is a mystery. The fact that this was a nurses' dorm may factor in.

During the CPI investigations in 2007, a former employee told us that she would not stay in Building 220 past six o'clock in the evening. She said that security forces' military police entered the building one night because they received a call that the door was open. Two of them were inside and getting ready to exit the building. They had M16 guns strapped across their backs. One of the men heard his gun handle charge—a clicking sound. They scurried out. They immediately checked the gun and discovered that there was a round in the chamber.

There were notes in our files that alluded to a bad romance in which the couple had a big blow up, and ultimately, one of them was thrown out of the window of Building 220.

TEMPORARY HOUSING

Crow Creek Inn, Antelope Inn and Temporary Lodging Facilities

Gwen worked the graveyard shift at the Crow Creek Inn. Here, the ghosts see fit to interact with the staff and the guests who experienced a variety of unusual things. Gwen felt someone walk up behind her one night as she was making photocopies in the back office. She turned to assist the person but saw no one, although she still felt the presence right beside her. Various women working at night at the Crow Creek Inn have reported hearing their names beings called out when they were alone. Mackenzie said she felt an invisible hand touch her neck.

Inexplicably, the electronic equipment—including the vacuum and coffee machine—would make unrecognizable sounds that they don't generally make, which caused alarm.

Frenzied guests said they saw a soldier riding on a horse down the main hall. People regularly reported seeing soldiers walk through their hotel rooms with no regard for their privacy. A man was innocently asleep in his hotel room. The television kept turning on and off, and then something brazenly ripped the covers right off of him. He was scared out of his wits and feared being accosted.

The "big" house is said to be haunted by "Bob," who makes noises and flushes the toilet in the inn when the cleaning staff is there, clearly wanting to be noticed. If they remove the pictures from the wall, they quickly discover that the artwork is mysteriously hung back up in its former spot.

A couple staying at the Antelope Inn was enthralled as they watched a medicine bottle roll across the top of the television. It went all the way to the right, stopped and then went all the way to the left—back and forth, back and forth. Then their soccer ball flew across the room as though someone had kicked it. They could feel the presence in the air. The husband claimed his skepticism in the paranormal was gone after a night at the inn.

The cleaning crew gets frustrated because when they have finished making up a room, the housekeeper signs off on the room but is frequently called back to find the bed a mess. Things move around, even when people are in the room. A noise is heard, and when the person turns around, he or she discovers something in a different spot.

I have been told many stories about temporary lodging facilities (TLFs) over the years. There is more than one temporary lodging facility on base, and the people who share their stories don't generally remember which building number they were in. An officer was staying at a TLF—he was new to the area and didn't know of any of the ghost stories of the building. He told his superior officer that when the guests would be in the sitting room watching TV, the drawers in the bureau would open and close by themselves. They would sit there and watch them open and then close…repeatedly. They inspected the drawers to see if there was any logical explanation but came up with none.

Henry and his wife had stayed at this same building. His wife overheard two of the housekeepers chatting. A man, who had been there the previous night, rushed into the billeting office in great distress. He said there had been a woman who was not of this world standing at the foot of his bed. Traumatized, he refused to ever go back into the building. The housekeepers had to gather up his belongings and bring them to him.

A story has been passed down in one of the temporary enlisted men's lodging buildings about cheating hearts that led to a couple being found hanged in the attic. The occupants hear footsteps coming from attic.

Jim, Jena and their four children stayed in a TLF for a week—a very long week by all accounts. The couple was overcome with a feeling of dread when they entered their assigned temporary quarters. They felt an especially heavy dread engulf them in the back two bedrooms. The pair immediately shut these two rooms and, without any explanation, instructed the children to sleep on the queen-sized sofa in the living room. Their baby slept between them during their stay. Jim and Jena struggled through the week without sleep—they were too spooked. Jena would recite a Bible passage each night with the hope that it would protect them from the foreboding evil that lurked there.

They had decided to keep the back bedrooms closed during their stay, but one of the doors kept opening on its own. Jena actually watched the doorknob turn and the door fling open with no human assistance.

Jena was so uncomfortable that when her husband went off to work, she would pack up all four kids every day and leave, trying to find things to occupy their day until Jim returned from work. She did not want any interactions with these energies and was desperate to get out of the TLF.

Jena finally fell asleep the last night they were there because she was completely exhausted. Jim was just dozing off when he felt her forcefully nudge him. Concerned, he looked over at her and saw that both she and the baby were sleeping. Neither of them could have been the one to disturb him. He nervously looked around but did not see anyone or anything.

When the couple finally prepared to leave the TLF and move into their permanent lodging, some of their personal items were missing. They were later found in the wrong suitcases. For example, the comb and hairspray were in the shoe bag. I am happy to report that they were assigned to a duplex for which I have no ghost stories.

A family of four was transferred to Warren from Texas in 2009. They spent their first four days in Cheyenne in TLF 2308 while waiting for their housing assignment. They continually heard children playing, but there weren't any kids in the building other than their own. They even heard children at 12:30 a.m. Agitated, the couple got up and looked around, intending to scold the loud youngsters, but found no one.

III
Businesses / Non—Housing

Original Entrance and Guardhouse

The original entrance to Fort D.A. Russell was located at the eastern point of the diamond that made up the original fort. Today, a large stone marker sits between two cottonwoods in Aisne Parade Field to mark the location. It was situated exactly three miles from town due to the regulation that alcohol was prohibited within three miles of a military installation. When the post was designated as a permanent installation, the gate was moved farther east to accommodate new officers' quarters and barracks. This is the same block where the charming dollhouses are located. The first guardhouse is shown on the map at the southern point of the fort—right in front of the headquarters building.

There is a well-known story of a security policeman who was making his rounds early one morning while most of the base was asleep. He was surprised by a soldier standing at attention under the murky streetlight. He approached the soldier to inquire why he was there. The clouds rolled in front of the moon, and he could no longer make out the man's figure. When the clouds moved through, the soldier had disappeared into the night air. This popular story is also told in Debra Munn's *Ghost on the Range* and is written up on several paranormal websites.

Actually, the current security force police tell me there are numerous sightings of a guard standing at attention at the original post entrance. The soldiers took their responsibilities very seriously; guarding the gate could mean life or death if there was a raid. The deep devotion and passion for their jobs has embedded itself here for all these years.

RANDALL AVENUE BRICKS

Now that we have explored the "other dimension" in the historic homes on Warren Air Force Base, let's take a peek into the business and administration facilities. Randall Avenue is the main street that runs the width of the post. The south side of Randall Avenue is uniformly lined with distinguished redbrick office buildings in proper military fashion—each with well-groomed grounds and mature trees. Care has been taken to keep the exteriors of the buildings historically correct. They were built from 1906 to 1910 as men's barracks. They are used for a variety of offices today.

TRAIL'S END

One of the first buildings is the Trail's End Club, where a 2007 bartender told of an unseen employee they'd dubbed George. He said the staff credited George with typing phantom drink orders into the bar computer. While these orders don't show up on the monitor, they do appear on the sales ticket, forcing the staff to be vigilant about checking each ticket before presenting it to the customer. George likes to play pool, dance, drink amaretto sours and stack up the shot glasses. I spoke to a current employee who feels like there is something there and experiences cold spots but nothing further.

HAIR-RAISING EXPERIENCE, COMMAND POST AND PUBLIC AFFAIRS, BUILDING 250

The Ninetieth Missile Wing headquarters is housed in Building 250, containing offices of the wing and vice commanders. This headquarters is the first historic brick building on Randall Avenue when you enter the base. It was built in 1910 as soldiers' barracks. The building was renovated in 1958 to accommodate these offices.

Ninetieth Missile Wing headquarters, Building 250, originally barracks. *Courtesy of Lisa Kindle.*

Years ago, a trolley passenger who was a major told his tour guide of an experience he had while working in this building. He and a female officer were the only people in the public affairs office. In compliance with military regulations, the female officer had her long, red hair pinned up. They were standing at a counter. He was resting his hands on the counter, and she was beside him typing on the keyboard. "Stop doing that!" she suddenly exclaimed. Stunned, he looked over at her and was dumbfounded to see her hair being pulled straight up into the air as though there were fingers pulling and running through it. Seeing his expression, she quickly realized he was not touching her. They were both thoroughly spooked by their visit from something beyond this physical realm. The major also told us that a cavalry soldier was killed in the basement there, implying that he was the tease.

A 2001 trolley passenger told the driver that the previous day she had gone up into the headquarters attic. She had been astounded to encounter a foggy entity floating right before her. It was free form—not in the shape of a human. She nearly jumped out her skin and quickly turned and dashed out of the attic.

In 2008, I was working with an airman from the public affairs office. The airman said that he had been in his office alone about seven o'clock in the evening. He went downstairs to the base newspaper so he could exit the building. The lights were already shut off for the night. As he descended the stairs, he heard two voices conversing. He paused for a moment, wondering who would be there chatting in the dark. When he was about halfway down the staircase, the talking suddenly ceased. What stood out for him was that the voices were speaking in an "old English" style—like he'd stepped a century back in time. There was no one down there when he reached the lower level. He searched the entire level looking for people, but to no avail.

FAREWELL

Captain Roger Elkins was intently working at his desk when he noticed someone was standing there. He looked up and saw Private Walker, who was supposed to be on a flight out of town. "What are you doing here?" the captain inquired. Without responding, Walker turned around and walked out. "That was odd behavior," the captain mused. As he stood up to follow Walker, his phone rang. It was then that Captain Elkins received the tragic news of the fatal plane crash 150 miles north of Cheyenne. This was the plane that Private Benjamin Walker was on. Mechanical failure was to blame for the crash. When Walker's effects were returned, the captain realized that the time on the soldier's broken watch was the exact same time that the ashen private had appeared in his office for a respectful farewell to his captain. I do not know which building the captain's office was in.

HANGING AROUND, BUILDING 248

After being stationed at Warren Air Force Base for eight years, Jake told our trolley drivers about Building 248. He said that the gory apparition of a man hanging in the attic often frightens people in this second brick building along the row. Jake said elusive shadow people flee through the boiler room. The shadowy figures disappear when they are followed. Jake opened an interior door of Building 248 after hearing a knock, but no one was in the hall. He stepped out into the hallway, but there was no trace of anyone left behind.

COMMUNICATION IS KEY, BUILDING 242

Building 242 is used for legal offices. After speaking with a base historian, I believe this story goes with Building 242. It was once an air police building, a jail and a communication building.

Charlie was a communication commander. When WAFB decided to renovate the old jail into a new communication command, Charlie took his family into the building to tour the old jail before it was changed. This would be his work facility once the renovations were complete. During the tour, his wife, Leslie, got a cold, tingly sensation, and then she felt a tap on her shoulder. She turned and looked around but saw no one. Lacey, their eight-year-old daughter, went up to the second floor. She turned left, and as she approached the first doorway, she was a bit surprised to see a man sitting behind the desk. She had thought her family members were the only people there. He smiled warmly and nodded his head to acknowledge her. Lacey politely said hello and continued down the hall. A few minutes later, the family was leaving the building, and her father went to lock the door behind them. Lacey told her dad not to lock the man in. He said there was no one else there, but she insisted that there was a man upstairs. Seeing his daughter was being truthful, Charlie went up to the office but found no one upstairs. Lacey was in a state of disbelief—she knew there had been a man inside.

DORA, CIVIL AIR PATROL, BUILDING 233

I accompanied Cheyenne Paranormal Investigations on an exploration of Building 233 in November 2007. It also did two follow-up investigations in 2008. Building 233 contains the offices for the Civil Air Patrol (CAP) and has been an administrative building for years. Originally, it stood beside the guardhouse, which was the jail. CPI decided this could be a captivating place to hold an investigation and was pleased to be granted access.

Step one in an investigation is to research the building, interview the residents and tour the location. We entered the historic two-story brick building. Inside, it still retains the sense of a home even though it has been used as an office for years. Mandy, a CAP employee, was there to host us. She seemed a bit tentative when we first arrived, but after a bit, she opened up, saying that while she was generally comfortable in her front office, there

Civil Air Patrol Building 233 was investigated by Cheyenne Paranormal Investigations. *Courtesy of Lisa Kindle.*

are times when she's there alone and she hears the sounds of coffee perking and then being poured into a cup. She can also smell it brewing.

The main floor includes a kitchen, two offices and a main room that was once the living room with a large staircase. Ascending these stairs, the upper floor contained three offices (former bedrooms), a bathroom and a community room, which is just used for storage. There's an open L-shaped balcony area around the captivating stairs.

In the dismal basement, they have a large meeting room that actually has an old coal chute. There's a sitting room, a boiler room and a storage room. Mandy admits that she hates being in the basement. She is required to attend a meeting down there once a month, and even though there's a group of people, she is extremely uncomfortable the whole time.

Once the equipment was set and the CPI team was in place, the investigators immediately had issues with their new camera batteries draining. A compass malfunctioned as well. The theory is that spirits draw energy off the equipment to manifest themselves. Once CPI left the property that night, the batteries were charged back up at the next location. During the second investigation at Building 233, the batteries also went dead, and the equipment was quite hot to the touch.

It is theorized that spirits can manipulate electromagnetic fields to draw energy. The electromagnetic field (EMF) readings were extremely high in the upper-floor restroom, where they also captured three EVPs (electric voice phenomenon), which are sounds conceivably created by spirits. One was of heavy breathing, another was of whispering and another was of sobbing. It's unusual for EMFs to be so high near a window, but CPI discovered a power line around the vicinity of the bathroom windows and feel that this could be the culprit for high EMF readings.

An investigator said he sensed something surrounding him, and then his hair had an electrical charge. Upon playing the audio back, they discovered an EVP of a dog's bark just as this happened. They noted several cold spots and even a breeze sweeping past them within the warm boiler room in the basement.

CPI recorded two more EVPs down in the basement. Trying to elicit a reaction, an investigator asked out loud if any spirit would like to identify itself. A female voice is heard on the audio tape saying, "Dora." During CPI's follow-up conversations with a colonel, he told them that a nurse named Doreen had been found deceased at the CAP building, but he was not comfortable elaborating on it.

I went through the cemetery records and found a Dora Decker listed. She perished on August 23, 1928, but I do not know the circumstances of her passing. I pulled these records from the RootsWeb and WAFB Grave Guide websites.

At the second investigation, the airman assigned to escort the team during its investigation and two CPI team members heard a male voice coming out of thin air. While the voice sounded as if it was coming from a distance, it was very distinct. The words came from the direction of the stairwell behind where the airman was standing. Later, they recorded a voice saying, "Who is that?" Several odd noises were noticed throughout the night, and at one point, a team member heard whispering emanating from the basement stairwell. While in the basement, they heard a loud thumping and clanging noise coming from the first floor. During the third investigation, Jessica and Scott both heard odd sounds and commented on it at the same time. Right then, the closed door at the bottom of the stairwell suddenly popped open, so Jessica took the EMF reader and swept the door. The EMF reader reacted with a constant blink, indicating a change in the energy field by the door; the previous EMF sweeps had indicated no activity.

Upon reviewing the audio data from the last investigation, CPI heard the recorded EVP saying "evil" twice during the night. Both times, the word was inserted between the team members' conversations. The two microphones were separated by a concrete wall. One was set up in the basement stairwell and the other in the conference room. The first EVP saying "evil" is considerably clearer in the microphone by the stairwell, and the second EVP is much clearer by the conference microphone, which is located on the other side of a wall, indicating that the entity that was speaking moved through the basement, from the stairs and to the conference room. CPI captured EVPs at the Civil Air Patrol Building during all three investigations there. In particular, the basement area seems to have significant paranormal activity. I was glad we were able to tap into the other side during these investigations.

LEGAL ACTION, BUILDING 232

Next to the Civil Air Patrol is another brick building, number 232, where legal offices are located. In 2007, I enjoyed visiting with Gene, a retired officer, who shared stories from working in Building 232. The building was an old barracks that was renovated into legal offices in 1992. During the renovation, they uncovered the pipes from the old potbellied stoves after removing the drop ceiling tiles. Graffiti left by cavalry soldiers was revealed.

The renovation seemed to spur the spirits. Gene said his co-workers were hearing footsteps pacing when they were alone in the building. One night, Gene was there by himself. He was locking up the building when he saw a guy in a buckskin jacket and a wide-brimmed hat with long, brown hair standing down the hall. What the heck was this guy doing here? Gene called out to him, but the man walked away from him. "Excuse me!" he hollered as he followed after him. "Excuse me!" he called again, but the man rudely ignored Gene. The man turned left and walked into one of the offices that was being remodeled. When Gene got to the door, he was surprised to find it was closed and locked. Upset that this unauthorized man was in the building, he pounded on the door. "Open the door; you're not supposed to be in here!" There was no response, so he took out his key and opened the door. The room was eerily empty and silent.

A colonel told us that she was working in this building at the late hour of one o'clock in the morning. She went into the first-floor women's bathroom, which is in the center of the building. While she was sitting there, she suddenly heard a loud scream in her stall, directly over her head. Scurrying to get out, she felt the presence leave the confined space. The colonel took a deep breath, trying to regain her composure.

Base Library, Building 214

Building 214 is a one-story, U-shaped facility, built in 1885 as infantry barracks for eighty-four men. They lived in large, dormitory-style rooms with metal-framed beds lining the walls. The library has been operating in this building since 1989. Besides having been barracks for the Twentieth Infantry, the building had also been a shooting range, a garden shop for the base exchange and a daycare center. Prior to 1989, the library was just next door in Building 213, which became the civilian personnel office.

I accompanied CPI on a paranormal investigation here in 2007. When we entered the library, we were standing in a large room with the checkout counter on the right and a children's reading circle on the left. There was a smaller room behind the checkout desk where the movie rentals are stocked. Continuing through the main room, we crossed through double doors into the large back room, which was lined with fully-stocked bookshelves. While investigating the library, Troy, Larry and Joe were in the back room, setting up equipment. Troy heard a book slam onto the floor. Joe said it just flew off the shelf right in front his face. Larry also heard the sound. Unfortunately, the equipment was not running yet, so it was not caught on tape or video. While taping in the room behind the checkout counter where the video rentals are kept, the team members could hear strange clanking sounds. The audio didn't catch the sounds but rather went from normal to white noise, as though they were in a wind tunnel.

In the science fiction section of the library, an employee saw an apparition of a cavalry soldier. The staff placed chairs in a circle in the children's section for story time. They often felt like someone was sitting there when no kids were around. While the team was in the children's library, their cameras, camcorders, an audio device and cellphones all turned off simultaneously. After a few minutes, they got the equipment turned back on again, at which time a couple of cellphones also rebooted.

Kim, one of our volunteers at the depot visitor center, had also worked part time at the base library. Kim said that the library staff often spoke of "George," their ghost. She said that long-term employee Lori had seen the books fly off the shelves numerous times. We'd heard many reports from various people over the years of books hurling off the shelves here. The manager told us that two cleaning ladies were in the building one night. One was cleaning up front in the lobby, and the other was in the back room where the majority of the books are shelved. She was vacuuming when an entire shelf of books shot out onto the floor directly in front of her. She frantically

Base library. *Courtesy of Lisa Kindle.*

ran up front and got her co-worker. Gathering their courage and holding onto each other's arms, they cautiously walked into the back room, where they saw that the books were in order back in their places on the shelf.

Another employee said that a man had hanged himself in this building; his misery is embedded here. She went on to say that John and Cliff, two cleaning men in the library, told her a menacing story. While working one night, John suddenly felt sturdy hands tighten around his throat. Unable to free himself, he was lifted up off the floor by a malevolent entity. Cliff, the second cleaning man, watched in horror. Terrified, he fled from the building. John was left to fend for himself, arms flailing at his unseen assailant. Things were beginning to go dark for John. The entity finally released John just before he passed out. John dropped to the floor, and the threatening being was gone. John still struggles to cope with his evil encounter.

BREAKING BREAD, BUILDING 266

Ron went into the small military-clothing store by the tracks in Building 266, which is situated just behind the library. He distinctly smelled the enticing aroma of fresh bread baking. Being friendly, he asked the staff, "Who brought in the home-baked bread?" They smirked and said no one had, but they are asked that a lot. The building was a bakery many decades ago.

TO DIE FOR, BUILDING 211

The small Building 211 was constructed in 1907. It served as a telegraph office at one time. The bars on the windows were added when it was turned into the paymaster's office. Times were different then—payday occurred whenever the paymaster made it safely back to the fort with the soldiers' wages, which was always a cause for celebration. Sometimes, the men went two or three months between pay periods. The law enforcement always had its hands full on payday. Libations flowed, and the pokey would be plumb full.

Building 211 also held the post barbershop. More recently, it was a museum, but today it is vacant. The story goes that a soldier went AWOL. He escaped and hid in or near Building 211, and soon he was captured and subsequently hanged. Since he met his doom, he is seen "hanging out" on the porch of the old paymaster's office. Maybe he had another paycheck coming to him.

ORIGINAL FORT HEADQUARTERS, BUILDING 210

Building 210 was erected in 1893–94 as the post command headquarters—the administrative facility for the entire post. The top floor was a large room used for activities such as dances, military ceremonies and theatrical productions and as a courtroom for court-martials. The building became the Warren Intercontinental Ballistic Missile (ICBM) and Heritage Museum for over thirty years, from 1967 to June 2013. Today, it is vacant and in need of renovations. The important history of Fort Russell and Warren Air Force Base resonates from this headquarters building. It stands in the southern apex of the original Fort Russell triangle.

The museum employees frequently encountered a cavalry officer from another dimension. They named him Jeffrey; he is seen in an 1880s cavalry captain uniform. I'm not certain if there was a reason they began calling

The first brick base headquarters, built in 1894, when the base was designated a permanent installation. It served as a museum for many years. *Courtesy of Lisa Kindle.*

him Jeffrey—if they know who he was when he walked the earth or if they just made up the name. Maybe Jeffrey subtly whispered his name into their ears when he made his initial appearances. He is not malicious in any way, but security forces have investigated the building more than once. They find the security system turned off and the door ajar in the wee hours of the night. The staff is positive they set the alarm before leaving and locked the deadbolt on the door. Sometimes, Jeffrey just turns the lights back on after everyone leaves, inviting another visit from security forces. One night, a museum patron approached the front door after the museum was already closed and locked up for the night. As the person neared the entrance, the door simply opened, welcoming him in.

Some of Jeffrey's shenanigans include turning the lights on and off, making the blinds go up and down, swinging the chandelier, rearranging the exhibits and pinching visitors' bottoms! In the morning, the ceiling fan chains are often found wrapped around the posts that connect the fans to the ceiling. The elevator was deemed inoperative because of the numerous times it stopped between floors with people inside. However, the maintenance crew was unable to find a problem. As in several of the historic brick buildings, the security dogs refuse to enter the attic.

An administrator at the museum set a cup and saucer on the table in the break room. She walked over to the counter, and when she returned, the cup had been turned upside down and the handle broken off. There was another woman in the room who witnessed this event. This volunteer decided to glue the cup and handle back together the following morning. When she went to the break room, she discovered the cup was intact.

Melvin, a base fireman, told us about receiving an alarm at the museum. Melvin went into Building 210 and turned on the lights, but he could not find anything out of order, so he cleared the alarm. The fire crew was sent back to the museum a second time because the alarm went off again. The crew hesitated to enter the museum; it thought a party was going on from the loud racket heard from outside. Of course, the men found the space empty.

This concludes our trek through the historic brick buildings situated along Randall Avenue. But wait—there's more! The majority of ghost stories told about the base refer to the old hospital.

HOSPITAL BUILDINGS

Where Death Comes to Life
Security Forces: Former Hospital Buildings 31, 34 and 37

The old hospital is located on the north side of the base, just above the staff circle. The staff circle is a round street that shoots off Randall Avenue where the medical corps lived. From there, they could be easily called on and quickly dispatched to the neighboring hospital.

The first hospital was built in November 1867, during the fort's first year, when it was thought that this was a just a temporary post. It was constructed of planed boards and tarred sheathing paper and lit by hanging kerosene lamps. Outside at the back of the hospital, they had a "dead house" where the deceased were placed to decay until they could be properly dealt with. The "dead house" is marked on Dr. Alden's base map, which he drew in 1870. This was eventually removed, but there's no doubt the space retains lingering energies.

Here's how one patient's fatal event unfolded. It was January 1878; many a gambling man was taking shelter in a dive called the Wine Parlor in town.

Base hospital, built in 1910. *Courtesy of WY State Archives.*

A dispute arose, and Long George pulled out his pistol. Officers arrived, and seven men were arrested. The following day, they were released from jail. Well, naturally, Long George headed straight back to the Wine Parlor. He and his cronies attacked a soldier who was leaving the saloon. Sergeant Moore heard his friend's desperate cries and ran outside to help, but he was also accosted. A ruffian grabbed his hat and ran, and Moore gave chase. Long George fired four shots at Moore, hitting him in the gut. The police nabbed Long George at the stable where he was attempting to saddle his horse and flee. Moore clung to life for one week before he perished at the Fort Russell hospital. Long George was sentenced to eight years in prison, but Governor Hoyt pardoned him after just three and a half years.

Brick Building 31 went up in 1887 after the base was designated a permanent military installation, replacing the makeshift wooden hospital building. The middle section is two stories, with single-story wings off the east and west sides. There were two wards with twenty-four beds in each ward. The building was remodeled in 1928 to house noncommissioned officers' families. Later, in 1969, it was vacated and boarded up, sitting empty until 2013.

Cheyenne Paranormal Investigations had hoped to investigate old Hospital Building 31, but at the time, the windows were all boarded up. The daunting building was slated to be condemned, and CPI could not get permission to enter. Five years later, the powers that be decided to save the building. They put some money and elbow grease into the

ICBM Heritage Museum in former Hospital Building 31. *Courtesy of Lisa Kindle.*

fading structure. It now houses the ICBM Museum. It's unfortunate that the general public does not have easy access to this museum because of security measures put into place since the tragedy of 9/11. The museum holds many historical treasures. The curator says there are no ghosts residing at the museum, but I'm not so sure. I heard a story that, during a renovation, the construction crew would put up boards and sheetrock, and the next morning when they'd arrive, they would find everything they had done the day before undone. Boards and sheetrock would be lying on floor. This project proved to be very frustrating for the crew, who had difficulty explaining why the renovations were taking so long.

More than a century ago, in 1910, the large Hospital Building 34 was completed to replace Building 31. Building 34 went up next door to Building 31. It is a hotbed of activity and certainly has the history to back it up. Any time I have a conversation regarding the paranormal activity on the base, people immediately mention the old Hospital Building 34 and all of the stories they have heard or personally experienced there. Many of the stories from here were told to me by more than one source. If ghosts linger near the place of their tragic end, it stands to reason that the hospital would be haunted. This is where death comes to life. There are numerous sightings of a red light seen here from the outside, but there are no red lights operating inside the building.

The hospital had room for 250 beds with a square footage of 41,100 above ground. Many of its patients and other inhabitants over the years have chosen to stay on. There are several reports of a matronly woman who would go room-to-room, opening the doors and peering in. It is believed that she was a nurse who is still checking on her patients, walking the path she once strode.

A doctor entity also presides here. He is most often encountered in the staff lounge. The employees feel a draft when he enters the room and when he swiftly passes by them. They see an impression in the chair directly in front of the television, just as though someone were sitting there, his weight indenting the cushion. He always changes the television station to medical shows. Items in the lounge were frequently rearranged to his liking.

It was common for patients to comment on the kind man who came to visit them. He would sit on the corner of their hospital beds and chat. They thought it was neat that he wore period clothing. The patients would tell the doctors and nurses to tell the elderly guy in the cavalry uniform thanks for the visit. However, there wasn't any living person who actually came to the hospital in this historic soldier's clothing. There were no employees or volunteers asked to do this. It is believed that he was the kind spirit of a cavalry soldier visiting from beyond—an eternal caregiver.

A sergeant saw this cavalry officer in the hallway one evening. The officer was adjusting his pant legs around his boots. The sergeant greeted him as he neared, and the soldier smiled as he replied, "Howdy." The soldier had a stripe down his pants like the 1800s uniforms did. As soon as the sergeant passed by him, he turned to do a double take, realizing that the man was somewhat transparent. There was no sign of the cavalry soldier; he had vanished without a trace.

Perhaps the worst account is one of a reliable watch-duty employee. She was found running out of the hospital screaming hysterically and stammering. She curled up in a ball on the ground, still stammering. All they could decipher was that she had seen something unnatural, not of this world. This employee did not recover from this incident. She went on permanent disability and was sent to a mental institution. I would be very skeptical of this account except for the fact that I know and respect one of the gentlemen who was there and tried to help her when it happened. This source was in charge of a law enforcement group at the base. He is a pillar in our community and not the type to exaggerate. He knew the woman, worked with her and is very saddened by her breakdown.

In September 1977, the new composite medical facility opened. Building 34 then became headquarters for the Security Forces Ninetieth Missile Wing, which is still housed there today. Even these seasoned military police officers get frightened inside this building. When Cheyenne Paranormal Investigations and I were allowed on the base to do some investigating, the hospital was the first place they requested access to. Unfortunately, there were too many people in the building to conduct a proper investigation, causing an increased possibility of inaccurate data. It did provide us the opportunity to interview several employees and learn of many anomalous incidents.

First Floor

Security employees working one night reported hearing a ruckus above them. It sounded as if furniture was scraping across the floor. Investigating, they found the room above them to be locked. They could not locate a key for this office. The next morning, a key was obtained, and when they opened the door, they found all of the furniture was stacked in the center of the room, piled all the way to the ceiling. Again, the ruckus was heard overhead late one night. This time, a key was on the premises. By the time they grabbed the key, ran upstairs and unlocked the door, half of the furniture was again stacked in the center of the room.

Randy, who was new at WAFB, tells of his first night working in Building 34. He was stationed at the law enforcement desk by the front door. People need to check in at the desk when they enter the building. At the beginning of the shift, Randy didn't know anything about the ghosts at the base. A security troop came running up to the window and asked if they had seen the "cavalry soldier with the horse." He skeptically looked over at the desk sergeant, then back at the guy and sarcastically said, "In the building?" Randy soon came to realize that the men in the troop were dead serious. He learned that there are many sightings of this soldier and his horse. He also heard from a few people who saw an "old man" sitting by the soda machines. The man would dissipate as the people got near. An enlisted man was spooked by the apparition that had materialized. It was a very pale man sitting on a garbage can beside the pop machine. He greeted the man but got no response, and then the apparition vanished before him, sending the man running back to his office, all the blood draining from his face. Working in Building 34 is not for the faint of heart.

Second Floor

The northeast wing is camper support, which used to be a children's ward. The northwest wing is response force.

In the 1800s, the hospital stewards were provided with apartments on the second floor of the hospital. In the late 1890s, there were two stewards, Unger and Frohwein. Emil Frohwein was known to be a true gentleman. He had served as an officer and a physician in the German army before coming to the United States. Frohwein lived in the second-floor hospital apartment along with his wife, Molly, and their four children. Two of these children perished—according to cemetery records, one was an infant. In 1889, Mr. Frohwein contracted yellow fever while serving in the Spanish-American War. It was his duty to care for patients in the war. He succumbed to the disease that he contracted from his patients. His casket was forwarded to Fort Russell. It was sealed tight with a label reading, "Not to be opened, contagious disease." His widow laid her husband and two of their children to rest in the Fort Russell cemetery.

A man who works in the camper support section told us that one night in 2001, he was there very late—two o'clock in the morning. He heard children playing and bouncing a ball. "That's crazy," he thought. He stood up and checked the hallways and neighboring offices. There were no children there, but he continued to hear kids playing. Then he realized this was where the children's ward once was. Apparently, many others have had similar experiences in this wing.

A soldier was working alone late at night in his office. The printer began making the clattering noises it makes when doing a print job, but he had not sent a job to this printer. Curious, he walked over to the printer. To his amazement, he discovered that the power was turned off.

Another man recounted a time when he was sitting quietly at his desk, deep in thought, and a board literally flew out of the ceiling with great force and nearly struck him. He was grateful that this menacing spirit had not injured him, but not willing to push his luck, he left the premises immediately.

One evening, a young girl was noticed at the end of the hall by a sergeant and another staffer. She was surrounded by mist. The men stopped and watched her as she stared back at them, and then she strode right through a wall. Astounded, the men rushed to the spot where she had disappeared; to their disbelief, she had vanished without a trace. They checked all of the nearby doors and found they were locked. This story has been previously published in the *Sentinel* base newspaper and in the captivating *Ghosts on the Range* book by Debra Munn.

Third Floor

This is where the classrooms and the communication room are located. There was a third-floor jail here at one time, and it used to be an emergency care area when the building was a hospital.

Footsteps and music drift down from the attic above when no one is up there to be accountable for the sounds. An employee we met during our investigation said that he was here working at three o'clock in the morning. He was typing up a report that was due the following morning. He kept hearing people walking in the hall outside his office, but he knew he was the only one there. Enthralled by the sounds, he would get up, go to the door and look both directions, but there was never anyone to be seen.

A group of men were chatting in the hallway. There are four sets of swinging bay doors that would open and close in this hall. As the men stood there, they could hear heavy boot steps tromping down the hall toward them and could even feel the floor reverberate. The doors in the hall opened and then closed, and they all felt a breeze as the entity passed by them. There were eight staff members to witness this. I was told this has actually occurred on several occasions. Sometimes, they could see the apparition, and it would come as close as six inches in front of them, then vanish directly before their eyes, taunting them. This story came to me from a respected former police officer.

Here's a story that has been previously published in the base newspaper and in *Ghosts on the Range*. A female sergeant was working alone on the third floor well after midnight. First she heard knocking and banging sounds on the walls surrounding her. This got her attention—she sat up straight, alert and listening, trying to figure out what was making the sounds. She felt the sensation of someone blowing on her neck and ears. She gasped, and the next thing she knew, the unseen entity kissed the nape of her neck! Hysterical, she radioed for help. The officers came charging in with guns drawn, ready for action, because she had sounded so frightened. Sometime later, another woman reported feeling the same sensation on her neck.

The spirit of the doctor I mentioned is often noticed in the lounge and in the patients' rooms. He is also attributed with the distinct sound of a jail door opening and closing of its own accord on the third floor. Then his footsteps can be heard echoing down the hallway. Sometimes, the footsteps would continue until the entity was directly in front of the witness. They have learned that they have to greet him before he will move on. When people were confined in the jail cell, their shoes were often gone in the morning.

They were generally found in another cell, lined up perfectly. This doctor's spirit feels quite at home in the third-floor doctor's lounge. He moves a chair directly in front of the TV. People can see an impression where he is sitting in the chair. He changes the channel on the television to his liking.

Hailey told me that she didn't believe in ghosts until she was seriously frightened one night, and she could not come to any other conclusion than that there was something paranormal here. Hailey worked in supply, which was on the third floor at that time. She said the last team had come in and dropped off all its supplies at her office door about seven o'clock that night. Hailey heard voices behind her office door as she approached, which she thought was strange. She cautiously opened her office door to a dim, empty room. She flipped on the light switch and carried the supplies into her office. Then she heard the voices again; this time, they were coming from down the hallway. She also heard footsteps striding down the hall and thought some of the team must not have left. Hailey walked out to the hallway to see who was there and again found herself alone. Now feeling really anxious, Hailey walked back into her office. She stopped in her tracks when she heard all of the doors on the third floor open. She was standing there wondering what was happening when all the doors loudly slammed closed at once. Fumbling, she locked her office door and ran down two flights of stairs. Her fear was palpable. She exited the building as fast as humanly possible. She is still trying to come to terms with what she experienced.

Fourth-Floor Attic

There are wings built off of the main section of the top floor. These wings are currently used for storage but were originally used as a mental ward where most thoughts were as dark as night. The doctors divided the patients by age groups and placed them into the different wings of the attic. The space still has wood-slat flooring, dormer windows and, like any old building, some water leakage. I generally love old spaces where I can literally feel immersed in the history. When touring or investigating old buildings, I rarely feel nervous, but this area gave me an underlying grim feeling. Its oppressive heaviness made me very uncomfortable and sick to my stomach, with a pressure in my head like a vice. Although the mental ward was not a small area, I felt claustrophobic and hurried to get out of the room. I am not easily shaken, so this really surprised me. Embarrassed, I really didn't want anyone to know how uncomfortable I was. The CPI team noticed an odd smell in one wing, and members also felt uneasy.

A chief master sergeant went into the attic area in 2001. He claimed that he heard three separate disembodied voices conversing. He could not decipher the chatter but was sure that there were three distinct voices.

When interviewing many security force officers over the years, almost every one of them spoke of the highly trained German shepherds that refuse to enter the attic or the morgue space. A dog actually attacked his handler when he attempted to take him into the attic. The forceful dog ran clear back down to the first floor. This dog wouldn't enter the third-floor jail either.

An easy-going friend of mine named Terry used to work in Building 34 for security forces. He worked on the first and second floors during his career. As he was entering the facility one night, he saw that the attic storage area had a light on. He asked Kayla, who was working at the front desk, who was up there. She said no one should be up there and handed Terry the key to go check it out but not without warning him that weird things happen up there all the time. Terry rounded up a senior airman, and they went up to the attic together. Terry unlocked the door. As he opened it, the door forcefully pushed back closed. The senior airman tried, and the door slammed back in his face as well. They heard banging noises coming from inside. They kept trying to get in to no avail. Eventually, they went back downstairs; Terry went outside and looked upward and saw the light go off.

Basement

In the basement, we found the old mortuary, which was converted into the armory, where weapons are stored. For security reasons, we were restricted from entering the armory. Other rooms downstairs include a supply room, the elevator control and a boiler room, which holds an entrance to a tunnel that led to Building 37, directly west of this one. In the early years, they would take the contagious terminally ill patients through the tunnel on gurneys. Cemetery records reveal that there were smallpox, yellow fever, scarlet fever and diphtheria outbreaks in the 1800s. That gurney ride must have felt like the green mile or being transported to death row, their life expectancy only a day or two. These individuals spent their last days on earth withering away in the neighboring Building 37. Once the patient passed on, the body was rolled back over to Building 34 through the tunnel to the mortuary in the basement of the main hospital, Building 34. Events that happen in a place make a lasting impression. I was told that the place where they burned the bodies still holds ashes in it because it's historical and they cannot be touched. The eerie tunnel entrance is right below where the elevator was later installed in Building 34.

There is no basement in Building 37, but you can see on the exterior east wall where there used to be an entrance that has been sealed off, presumably where the tunnel led into the building. The patients were rolled into Building 37 from the main hospital. It is safe to say that numerous folks died under the roof of Building 37, so it's quite surprising that they report very little paranormal activity. Today, this facility houses special forces investigations; it was also used as an ophthalmology clinic for many years.

CPI and I were investigating both buildings in 2007; we were in the elevator control room down in the basement of the main hospital, Building 34. This is a particularly eerie area and definitely sets the mood for a ghost hunt. I was standing beside two of the team members taking in my dim surroundings. They both snapped pictures on their digital cameras. At the same time, they both exclaimed, "Wow!" I looked at their camera screens and saw that they had both caught a photo of a dense, free-form, white mist that had not been visible to the naked eye. The technical term for this mist is electroplasm. They snapped a few more photos that also showed the distorted, unnatural mist. The dreary basement space certainly felt inhabited, and the air felt electric.

Workers in the basement have sworn that as one walks down the hall at night, lights will turn off behind them. The basement workers have also heard the rattling sound of gurneys rolling past.

As a control measure, there is a doorbell at the entrance to the supply room that the staff must ring when they wish to order supplies. It is a simple doorbell with a two-syllable "ding-dong" tone. Occasionally, with no viable explanation, the bell will actually play a real song. It is a simple doorbell, not programmed to play tunes and should not be capable of doing this. They have changed the batteries when this happened, thinking maybe it somehow did this because the batteries were low, but it still played songs. Like the attic, the canine unit dogs won't enter the morgue area.

A retired officer from security forces told me that in the 1990s, the security forces put on a haunted hospital event one Halloween, which they held in this basement. Even though we've covered all the floors in this building, we are not quite done. Unusual things happen in yet another space in the building—the elevator.

Elevator: A Scare in the Air

The elevator is installed right at the tunnel entrance where they transported the terminally ill to Building 37 and then brought the corpses back into this building before decomposition set in. When people ride the elevator, it often feels as though they are being shoved out once the doors open.

During our CPI investigation in 2007, one of the men who worked on the second floor said he'd been told of four separate encounters where a calvary colonel appeared in the elevator and actually spoke to the passenger. With nowhere to escape to, the passengers panicked and rushed out the second the doors opened, hearts racing.

For the elevator's last run, an officer stepped into the elevator on the third floor, but then the doors opened again. He felt the chilling sensation of another person enter the small, enclosed space. While he could not see anyone, he physically felt an invisible mass shove him over to the side. The doors closed, and he couldn't get out. He desperately pushed the "open" button to no avail. Paralyzed with fear, he broke out in a sweat. With no choice, he rode down to the first floor with the unfriendly entity, trying to grasp what was actually happening. The officer barged out of the elevator the second the doors opened. He ordered that this elevator be locked and never used again. That order is still in place today.

Cavorting with Ghosts, Building 65

Jim was standing at the front counter in Building 65, the Twentieth Air Force Post Headquarters. This building sits near the cemetery. It was originally built as hospital barracks for 127 men of the Twentieth Medical Airborne unit in 1908, but the post commander took it for his headquarters, saying it was too nice for barracks.

There was an officers' club on the upper floor beginning in the 1930s. Jim was speaking to a woman who was working there when out of the corner of his eye, he saw a man and woman walk past in the hall. He turned and saw that the man was wearing a vintage formal uniform, and the lady was in a ball gown. Jim asked the woman at the counter, "Is there a costume ball tonight?" Realizing the improbability of what he had just seen, he said, "Never mind," but the impression stuck with him. The following year, another individual heard music and dancing coming from upstairs when no one was up there. Could this be the location where the couple had danced their last dance?

SOUTH BEND

The following stories reference historic buildings that are found south of the main thoroughfare.

Lead a Horse to Water: Youth Center 919 and Bowling Center 303

The youth center used to be located in an old World War II prefab building; this facility was razed many years ago. While still standing, it also housed a quartermaster shop and an airman's club called Breakers. The building was located where the parking lot east of Bowling Center 303 is now. It was in this building that the ghost of the cavalry officer was frequently seen leading his saddled horse down the hallway. The pair would turn left and then walk right through the solid wall, leaving witnesses with their jaws agape.

Inside of the bowling center, the staff members frequently see an apparition they call George. He is observed walking down one of the bowling lane aisles. An employee I talked with said he saw him early in the morning, and George was wearing a gray jumpsuit. Some of the other employees say they have seen him in a blue jumpsuit and have seen him at night as well. They have the impression that he's an older man who is dutifully working on the lanes.

Shed New Light, Building 367

Building 367 was built to hold supplies that were unloaded along the railroad. In the 1990s, it became the offices for civil engineers of the natural and cultural resources department and is now the missile engineering department.

An employee in this building told us of a lingering departed soul. In a rut, a soldier became bored of collecting the mail from the trains and performing the same monotonous duties day after day while existing in the middle of the sparse and windy prairie. His misery progressed, and he eventually succumbed to his dark depression and hanged himself in the elevator shaft.

The employee who shared this information works in Building 367. After shutting off the lights and leaving his office for the evening, he would frequently have to return to his locked office and once again shut off the lights. The spirit wants to brighten his world.

Airman's Attic Store, Buildings 347 and 341

The Airman's Attic is currently set up in Building 341 but was previously in Building 347. A current staffer says that when she returns in the morning, she finds things on the floor or in different places than where she left them. She admits that she does not stay there by herself, especially after nightfall. She gets a weird feeling in the space and says it seems like she is not alone.

I was told several stories about the previous location of the Airman's Attic in Building 347, mostly from security forces patrolmen. A couple of these law enforcement officers were dispatched to the Airman's Attic at three o'clock in the morning due to a disturbance. They went into the basement, where they jerked the closet door open to see if someone was hiding within. Instead, they found the ogling eyes of several dolls staring back at them. That's when they heard what sounded like a "three hundred pound" person walking right above them. Scurrying up the stairs, they found no one in their continued search of the building.

Another MP told me he saw two pictures that were taken in the attic with apparitions appearing in each of the photos. One displayed the silhouette of a woman in a long Victorian-style dress. The second was an ominous man with red eyes.

Boo! Building 321

Civil engineer squadron Building 321 is also located on Fifteenth Cavalry Road. It contains the building and grounds department. The ghost of a young girl about nine years old with long, blond hair gets into the spirit on Halloween. She turns off the locker room lights and jumps out from a locker or behind a corner to spook her unsuspecting victim. Next door in Building 320, the offices for civil engineers, footsteps from the empty floor above them can be heard at night. Security forces has been called to investigate to no avail.

Fire Station, Building 324

Down the street, the crew at the fire station on Warren Air Force Base told trolley driver Bill Green that the station is built atop an Indian burial ground. Melvin was a dispatcher stationed there in 1991. He speaks of an autumn night when the crew—consisting of a driver, the crew chief and two hand-

Fire Station 1. *Courtesy of Lisa Kindle.*

line men—were sitting in the dayroom at nine o'clock in the evening. The station was locked up for the night, and since it was fall, darkness had already settled in. Glancing off to the side, Melvin saw in his peripheral vision a Native American in a full, colorful headdress walk down the hall, seemingly lost in time. The spirit roamed into one of the fire truck stalls. Another crew member exclaimed, "Did you see that?" None of them dared to go check the stall for the first nerve-wracking seconds, but they gathered their courage. When they approached the truck stall, the Native American was gone. They had a brush with a presence from Wyoming's savage beginnings.

Melvin said that in 1868, the firehouse was a livery station, going on to say that this was also where they hanged the deserters. There were a lot of deserters, according to the history books. It was a gritty existence here on the naked prairie.

At three o'clock in the morning, Melvin heard chains rattling upstairs. This was a common occurrence, and all the crew had experienced it. He envisioned shackled prisoners whenever he heard the clanking sounds. The crew called their ghost Willard.

One pleasant evening in 1992, a fireman was sitting in front of the station, chatting with his wife, when they both vividly saw a cavalry officer and a few women in long dresses casually walk by right in front of them and then vanish, their days on earth timeless.

One very frightened crew member said he saw ghosts emerging from the ceiling in his room. He never again slept in his assigned room over the next four years that he worked there. He always slept in the chairs in the dayroom. Something can often be heard walking around from above, and when the firemen come back after a call, they find attic lights have been turned on while they were out. No one ever wants to go up there with the ghost, so they always send the new guy up to turn the lights off.

STABLES

Horsing Around, Building 340

A good friend worked in Building 340 for many years. This building is used as a commander squadron but was originally built as a stable when the fort was initially established. The stables were lined up on Fifteenth Cavalry Road. My friend said that the staff would sometimes hear horse sounds inside this

Veterinary hospital, Building 329. *Courtesy of Lisa Kindle.*

building. The reality of what happened in this location is horrific. The stables that originally stood here were used for Companies I and J of the Second Cavalry. The building went up in a huge inferno within a year of establishing the fort. It was the spring of 1868. The blaze could not be contained or controlled—they did not have a central water system until 1884. Tragically, sixty-five horses perished. Besides the devastating loss of the animals' lives, the horses and mules were their only means of transportation.

Fenced In, Building 336

A security guard was patrolling the fenced vehicle lot of the neighboring Building 336, another old stable. It was two o'clock in the morning when he heard chattering voices and people walking directly in front of him. Although he could not see anyone there, the voices cut through the night air. This was very disturbing to the officer; he wondered how he could combat something he could not see. Fortunately, it did not come to that—the voices faded away, and he reluctantly moved on.

A Stable Environment, Building 329

Built in 1908, Building 329 is the only horse stable and veterinary hospital that has retained its original design, keeping the original cobblestone floor and the forty-three stalls. The large facilities on this block stabled hundreds of army horses and mules. The other, smaller buildings held the tack. Building 329 was the home of the military dogs during World War II. They used the horse stalls as dog runs.

The Fifth Cavalry Reorganized moved into the authentic space. The building retains its original skylights two stories over the vet's operating room. The skylights were designed to roll open using a chain pulley system. Twenty years ago, the director of the Reorganized Fifth Cavalry told us this story.

Soon after the building went into service, the chain system failed. The doctor took it upon himself to shimmy up a pole. Perilously leaning out to reach the chain for the skylight, he lost his balance and plummeted to his untimely death. He lay motionless on the cobblestones.

No record of this perilous accident can be found. The legend says the accident was unauthorized and covered up. The staff of the Fifth Cavalry Reorganized calls the deceased veterinarian Casper, since there is no record of his name. There are notes in our files that in 1915, a trooper was stomped to death by a horse here.

Casper is credited with letting horses out of their stalls, turning the furnace on and off, opening and closing the basement door and rearranging the Christmas decorations.

The base maintenance crew was called to repair the boiler. When they tried to enter the basement, the door would not open. People had been locked in the basement several times, but there wasn't even a doorknob, just a hole where one used to be. They would prop the door open but find it closed when they returned. After this happened to the maintenance crew a second time, they decided to install a phone in the basement so no one would get trapped down there. The communications team laid the phone lines out where they were to be installed. They stepped outside to check the box, and when they went back inside, they found the wires neatly rewound back onto the spools.

A maintenance man who was downstairs by himself said that while repairing the boiler, a tool he needed was simply handed to him.

ARCHAEOLOGICAL CENTER AND FAMCAMP

There is a small archaeological center on the west side of the base. They have found evidence of Native American life here from as far back as 11,500 years ago. Next to that is FamCamp, where visiting military families can stay and camp on the base. When Fort Russell was established, this is where the laundresses' homes were located. They resided in shoddily constructed log huts that were about ten feet by eighteen feet and placed along the creek bank. It was called Suds Row. Initially, the military allowed a laundress for every one hundred soldiers, but that number gradually decreased to one for every twenty men. Some were the wives of the enlisted men or became wives during their time here since the men greatly outnumbered the women. In 1874, the powers that be ordered the laundress quarters to be vacated while they were disinfected because of a scarlet fever epidemic. Acid fumes were burned to kill the bacteria, and then the walls were whitewashed. In 1878, the funding for the laundresses was cut off. If they were married to an enlisted man, they were allowed to serve until his term was up.

They uncovered an old fire pit at FamCamp that has been dated at 1,600 years old. A base historian told me they found a Native American skull here in the 1940s.

FamCamp, where the spirit of a Native American woman is often seen and heard screaming. *Courtesy of Lisa Kindle.*

There is a well-known story of a Native American woman who was cruelly raped and terrorized, reportedly by a group of cavalry soldiers at White Crow Creek, which is where FamCamp is today. Many people have beheld the apparition of this desperate woman, hearing her heart-wrenching screams coming from the darkness of her soul. They can feel her sadness and desperation engulf them. The military police have been called over on several occasions. Men in the nearby barracks often report hearing these horrific screams. Although officers have heard her piercing cries of despair and inspected the bushes where she has been seen, they've never found anyone when examining the scene. Sounds become more prominent in stillness, and her screams cut right through you. When you run toward the screams, the direction of the cries seems to change, and you never find your victim.

I spoke of a military policeman named Randy earlier in the Building 34 section. He said he knows another MP who responded to the anguished moans heard at FamCamp. Randy described the man as one of the most serious, no-nonsense people he knows. Randy asked him about the incident, but he didn't want to talk about it, other than to say he couldn't explain any of it but that something paranormal really happened.

Eve had a summer job updating the cabins at FamCamp. Her duties included painting and wallpapering the rustic cabins. It was a hot August day. Eve was kneeling on the floor in the bathroom, working with the wallpaper. Suddenly, she was enveloped in coldness, as though she were wrapped in a sheet of ice. Shuddering, she then felt something touch her shoulder, which really startled her because she was alone in the room—or so she had thought. A moment later, her supervisor came to the doorway. Seeing the expression on her face, he asked if she was OK. Embarrassed, she said she was fine, but in truth she was completely unsettled. The chill lingered as she tried to make sense of the events.

CEMETERY: SPIRITS IN THE AIR

The picturesque base cemetery is located on the northeast side of the post. This is the final resting place for over 850 departed military personnel and their family members. These were people who lived, loved and laughed here on the post. "Unknown" marks 34 of these graves. Private John W. Saunders was the first decedent to be buried here in December 1867. There is a section in the southeast corner that contains the remains of 10 prisoners of war. These POWs were restrained at the base, but in all actuality, they were treated very well. Country representatives have attended memorial services in their honor. The German embassy has sent money for flowers to be placed on the graves in celebration of the German memorial day (Totensonntag) in November.

While examining cemetery records, I noticed the following causes of death: killed in a brawl, run over by a wagon, struck by lightning and delirium tremens while under arrest. It was shocking to see the number of children in the listings. There were many deaths from a scarlet fever epidemic in 1871. Smallpox reached epidemic levels at the fort and in Cheyenne in 1877. Fort residents were not allowed into town during these times in an effort to prevent the spread of the diseases. George Little Tail was an enlisted man who joined after the hostilities. He passed away in February 1893. A guard was murdered by the prisoner he was overseeing. Just as his funeral was ending, a posse came bearing the deceased corpse of his assailant. They placed the murderer in the open ground without

Graves of those who lived, laughed and loved at WAFB. *Courtesy of Lisa Kindle.*

a flag-draped casket and covered his limp body with dirt; he received no ceremony or honors from his peers. His body remained there for three weeks until his family retrieved it for a proper burial.

One decedent was listed as a female Philippine servant in 1912. German POW Ludwig Winter killed himself when he learned that Hitler was dead. There were a few listing of the laundresses—one committed suicide with a gun. I noted two listing for buglers. In 1871, Sergeant John Limeburner, Company D, Fifth Cavalry, met his doom from a bullet wound received at a brothel halfway between Cheyenne and Fort Russell. Military comrades purchased him a headstone, grave B-25aa. Grave C241 contains the remains of two unknown soldiers. Grave D320 lists "Indian skeleton found on base in 1943." There are a couple of small fenced-in graves of mascots—beloved dogs that were honored here as well.

In 1979, the strategic air command closed the cemetery for future burials. Reservations were taken for the remaining plots, but they did not expand the grounds. Some of the spirits wander the grounds here at the cemetery. Civilians, military personnel and security police have reported seeing spectral images of fallen soldiers at this cemetery for decades. Remnants of lost spirits linger on at the graveyard.

Dying to get in. *Courtesy of Lisa Kindle.*

Over twenty years ago, a trolley passenger approached Val after a base historical tour. We had not started doing ghost tours yet. She told Val that she was a certified medium, but how and where do mediums get certified? Is there an online program? Certainly not twenty years ago. Joking aside, I do believe some people are able to tap into their sixth sense and grasp things the majority of us can't. The lady said that when the trolley traveled by the base cemetery, she had seen the aura of "spirit ladies" putting flowers on the grave sites and walking among the dead. I can envision these ladies somberly roaming among the headstones in the stillness of the night.

One of the frequently reported phantoms seen is that of a mourning woman wearing a black veil and dress. She is observed at the graves late at night, grieving—her misery palpable. Several security police have seen her from afar, but when they approach her, she disappears. No traces of her remain in her absence.

An officer was patrolling the area and neared the cemetery. As he rounded the curve, he shone his spotlight over the grave markers. The patrolman saw two cowboys leaning against a headstone. Thinking this very odd, he pulled over and jumped out of his car, accidentally dropping his flashlight.

He bent over to pick up the light and then turned the light beam to the area where the cowboys were standing. They had vanished, and he could find no footprints in the freshly fallen snow. He examined the headstone; the date of death inscribed was 1889. Throughout his service, he continued to drive past the cemetery, but he never saw the two cowboys again. Val was originally told this story by the officer, but it was also written up in Debra Moon's *Ghosts on the Range.*

A group of fourth-grade girls were at a slumber party hosted at a home on the base in 2008. The rambunctious girls enjoyed an evening of snacks, giggles and ghost stories. They told the ghost stories they'd heard about the base, especially the scary tales about the cemetery. Ashley, one of the girls, said that her grandmother was buried in the cemetery. She said that she had died from the Spanish flu. Liking to play with things that scared them the most, they snuck out in the black of night, slinking off to the cemetery for a spooky adventure. Each girl was armed with a walkie-talkie for their covert investigation. Bravely, they split up, each taking a different section of the ominous cemetery. They got more of a scare than they bargained for. While staked out, they heard Ashley's blood-curdling scream, panicking as she sprinted across the cemetery. They chased her down the street. Finally she stopped running; she was trembling and emotionally overwhelmed. Breathlessly, she told her friends that the spirit of her grandmother—"only with a devil face"—had chased her and screamed, "Get out, get out!"

CONCLUSION

Fort Russell has been through some drastic changes over the years. It developed in the nineteenth century among the Native Americans and western pioneers and is still operating in this twenty-first-century age of nuclear missiles. During this entire time, the one thing that has been consistent is the devotion to our country of the numerous soldiers who have

That's all, folks! *Courtesy of Lisa Kindle.*

lived and served here. This devotion may be the reason that many of these spirits have remained at the post, continuing to protect us.

I've shared with you nearly all of the paranormal encounters we've heard about the base, covering about sixty residences and over twenty businesses on WAFB, but I'm sure there are hundreds more stories to be told. I would love to hear any experiences you've had or have heard about if they are not recorded here. I continually gather people's accounts of the paranormal for Cheyenne and Warren Air Force Base.

Living at WAFB often turns skeptics into believers of the great beyond. The continual interactions with those who have passed on give us glimpses of eternity and what it holds. I like to believe that we will have the ability to oversee our loved ones from the other side and travel through layers of time and dimensions, giving us the ability to watch the future generations of our family grow.

References

Books

Adams, Gerald M. *Fort Francis E. Warren and the Quartermasters Corps in World War II, 1940–1946*. Fort Collins, CO: Citizens Printing Inc., 1994.

———. *The Post Near Cheyenne: A History of Fort D.A. Russell, 1867–1930*. Boulder, CO: Pruett Pub. Co., 1989.

Cheyenne Centennial Committee. *The Magic City of the Plains, 1867–1967*. Cheyenne, WY: Centennial Committee, 1967.

Fleishman, Martha, and Carol Joy Justice. *Bugs to Blizzards, or An Army Wife at Fort D.A. Russell*. Cheyenne, WY: Wigwam Press, 1974.

The History of Cheyenne, WY. Vol. II. State Historic Preservation Office, 2009 Year in Review. [Page 74 article by Edward Tarbell, and pages 105–09 written by James Harrell; page 105 article by Mike Cook, USAF Twentieth AF.]

Munn, Debra D. *Ghosts on the Range*. Helena MT: Riverbend Publishing, 2008.

O'Neal, Bill. *Cheyenne: A Biography of the Magic City of the Plains, 1867–1903*. Austin, TX: Eaken Press, 2006.

Taylor, Paula Bauman. *F.E. Warren Air Force Base*. Charleston, SC: Arcadia Publishing, 2012.

WEBSITES

Haunted Hotspots. FamCamp. http://www.carpenoctem.tv/haunt/wy/ (accessed 2006).

Oral Cancer Foundation. Sammy Davis Jr. http://www.oralcancerfoundation.org/people/sammy_davis.html.

RootsWeb. rootsweb.com/pub/usgenweb/wy/laramie/cemeteries/fewarren.txt (accessed 2007).

State Historic Preservation Office. http://wyoshpo.state.wy.us/pdf/MilitaryContext.pdf.

Warren Air Force Base. www.warren.af.mil.

NEWSPAPERS

Adams, Gerald. "No Military Airfield Now—But We Did Have a Dandy." *Sunday Tribune Eagle*, December 7, 1980.

Airman's World, October 2001.

Cook, Mike. Article on Quarters 92. *WY State Historic Preservation News, Year in Review* newsletter, 2009.

Johnson, Bert. Article featuring Debra Munn. *Warren Sentinel*, 1980.

Lanham, Chuck. *Tales from Cheyenne, The Military—Yesterday and Today*. Newsletter, February 2007.

Lynd, Roy F. Fort D.A. Russell article. *Recruiting News*, 1924.

Letter

Spring, Agnes Wright. Agnes was appointed Wyoming state librarian and state historian in 1916. Letter written to Colonel Gerald M. Adams, USAF (retired) and author, June 16, 1983.

Brochures

F.E. Warren Archeology Center brochure.

Tarbell, Edward. F.E. Warren AFB Cemetery Grave Guide, 1996.

Warren ICBM & Heritage Museum brochure.

Warren Spouses Annual Historic Homes Tour, Fort Russell Days brochures, 1995, 1997, 2010.

Tours

Cheyenne Paranormal Investigations and base escorts, 2007.

Lyon, Dan. Escorted tour, 2009.

Ornella, Christen. Escorted tour, 2014.

Warren Air Force Base Audio Tour. The audio tour can be accessed by cellphone while driving the route inside the base. 2007.

Personal Accounts from Base Residents

This is where the majority of the information written in the book is derived from.

About the Author

Jill Pope is the director of operations at Visit Cheyenne Convention and Visitors' Bureau. She has managed and co-written the Cheyenne Street Railway Trolley ghost tours for twelve years. These popular tours sell out each year, with some customers traveling from neighboring states to experience the tours. It is Jill's passion to document people's spiritual encounters in Cheyenne, Wyoming, and the surrounding area—delving into

the history of the haunted locations and making sense of the paranormal experiences that occur there. Over the past seven years, she has collaborated with a few paranormal investigation teams to meld scientific explorations with people's experiences and lore. Some of the stories she tells have been passed on for years, while many were relayed directly to her by the individual who experienced the recent paranormal event.

Jill wrote *Haunted Cheyenne* in 2013 as part of The History Press's Haunted America series and went on to spin her ghostly tales of the paranormal activity within the gates of Warren Air Force Base, located on the western edge of Cheyenne, Wyoming.

Jill is also an artist, using several mediums, including sculpting, stained glass and painting. Her work can be seen on the streets of Cheyenne, where two of her eight-foot-tall painted fiberglass boots are displayed in the depot plaza. The boots are part of the "These Boots Are Made for Walking" city-wide collection. The names of Jill's boots are *Don't Feed the Animals* and *Milestones, the Chamber of Commerce's 100th Anniversary Boot.*

Jill is married to Darin Pope and is the mother of two children (Heather and Brady) and three stepsons (Tyler, Justin and Austin). She also has two grandchildren—Jaidyn and Hagen. All of them own her heart.